REVELATION
A Novel

Gary McCarragher

Revelation, published January, 2023
Editorial and proofreading services: Cath Lauria, Gina Sartirana
Interior layout and cover design: Howard Johnson
Photo Credits: Front Cover Image: Abstract self portrait, by Christian
Beirle González; Image #100005105, Getty Images.
Author Photo: by Terry Sbani, Woodside's Photography Studio.

 **SDP Publishing**

Published by SDP Publishing, an imprint of SDP Publishing Solutions, LLC.

ISBN-13 (print): 979-8-9862833-2-6

ISBN-13 (ebook): 979-8-9862833-3-3

Library of Congress Control Number: 2022914940

Printed in the United States of America

Dedication

To Dr. Bart D. Ehrman

Acknowledgments

I would like to thank Angela van Barneveld, Erin McCarragher, Susan McCarragher, Jennifer Cochran, and Kent Patterson for their suggestions and encouragement. I'd also like to thank my editors, Cath Lauria and Gina Sartirana, for their fine contributions, and my publisher Lisa Akoury-Ross, for her support and guidance.

I would especially like to thank Dr. Bart D. Ehrman, the James A. Gray Distinguished Professor at the University of North Carolina at Chapel Hill, for his valuable contribution. Dr. Ehrman has inspired me to heights I could have never imagined. I consider our extensive collaboration to be the highlight of my career as a writer. With deep respect and appreciation for his immense scholarly expertise, patience, and generosity, I dedicate *Revelation* to Dr. Ehrman.

The eyes of reason are the eyes of nature, and the eyes of nature cannot see into that which is beyond or above nature.

—John Pulsford
Quiet Hours

Reason is man's instrument for arriving at the truth ...

—Erich Fromm
The Sane Society

A bright Friday morning sun, unusually warm for early spring in Chapel Hill, peeked above the oaks, shortleaf pines, and red cedars of the verdant North Carolina landscape and streamed through Bart Trask's car windshield. He lowered the visor and headed for the Raleigh-Durham Airport. The prospect of having to face his twin brother, James, and especially his Baptist minister father, Pastor Theodosius Trask, tightened his insides. He had prepared a few remarks, a sort of explanation to soften the blows, but it did little to settle his queasy stomach.

As he started on the familiar flight south toward his child-hood home of Traskville, Alabama, named after his remark-able great-grandfather John Trask, he tried not to imagine the look on their faces. He considered forgetting his crazy idea, but he knew that he couldn't possibly do that. As if driven on by some force, the invisible puppet strings of his nature that he could neither resist nor fully understand, he moved forward.

He rolled down the windows, turned up the music, and stepped on the gas.

Bart pulled off the old country road into the Trask driveway, a wide semicircular path wrapping around an enormous laurel oak casting shade over his childhood home. The plantation house, fronted by a two-tiered veranda, white columns, black shutters, and a rooftop observatory, gleamed in the bright late afternoon sun.

His car came to a stop on crackling woodchips next to a wooden swing hanging from a limb of the massive oak, the same wooden swing on which his brother, their sister Junia, and he had spent many a carefree childhood afternoon. He shuffled his feet in the woodchips, ran his hand over the thick, weather-beaten rope holding the swing, and smiled wistfully.

He glanced at the church to the right of the Trask home, a beautiful, red brick High Victorian Gothic structure built in 1905 by his great-grandfather. Over the years Bart had developed a fascination with the architecture, featuring a pair of three-story towers, a cone-shaped roof with gothic arched vents, and stained-glass windows. Through many a Sunday church service he'd marveled at the care and craftsmanship that went into its construction.

He turned toward the house and took a deep breath.

After nearly twenty years of contentious "discussions"

with his father, starting in his mid-teens, intensifying during his years at Yale Divinity School where he earned an M.A. in Religious studies followed by his PhD in New Testament studies, and continuing through his years as an Assistant Professor at UNC in Chapel Hill, a truce had finally been declared about a year ago. During all subsequent family gatherings both Bart, the "agnostic from birth," and his father, the conservative evangelical Christian, had promised to avoid the subject. This did have the desired effect of making things generally more pleasant, but Bart could see in his father's eyes an ongoing, quiet despair over his lost son.

His mother, Linda, greeted him on the veranda with open arms and a loving smile.

"How are you, my son? Long time no see."

Bart returned a loving smile. For just an instant, the weight of his concerns lightened. "I'm fine, Mom. How are you? How is everybody?"

"Just fine. Wait until you see your little nephew. He's grown so big since Christmas. What a joy he is."

They entered the house. "Your brother is upstairs. Father is out back somewhere. Junia and little Thomas will be over shortly. Go on upstairs and settle in."

Bart turned toward the familiar thud of boots on the creaking front steps. A moment later his father appeared. "Well look who we have here, our long-lost son," he said, expressionless. "How are things up in Chapel Hill?"

Bart's stomach tightened. "Just fine. Yourself?"

"Better than I deserve. Mother, have you seen my reading glasses?"

"No. You probably left them in the church, dear."

Bart headed for the stairs. He found his brother lying on his bed, reading. He knocked on the open door.

James lowered his book. "Hey."

Bart smiled and entered. "How's it going?"

"It's going," James said, shrugging.

"Anything new and exciting in your life?"

"Not really."

"How's Emily?"

"We broke up a couple of months ago."

"I'm sorry to hear that. What happened?"

James tossed his book on the bed. "I don't know. I think she found somebody else. It's just as well. Anything new with you?"

The time had come, at least with his brother. Despite his preparation, he hesitated.

Just start talking.

"As a matter of fact there is. A couple of things."

James sat up. "You and Sarah are getting married."

Bart smiled. "Not exactly. At least not yet. I've still got you locked up for Best Man, right?"

James smirked. "We'll see. So, what's your news?"

Bart sat on his own bed across the room. "I've begun work on a new book, my first for a general audience."

"New book? On what?"

"The working title is *Jesus, The Man They Called God. The exaltation of a Jewish preacher from Galilee.*"

"The man they *called* God?" James took a deep breath. "I think I'll pass."

"I know, and that's okay. It's really just about the life and times of Jesus. It's amazing how little the average Christian really knows about him. There are some books out there for a general audience, but nothing like what I have in mind."

"Have you told Father?"

"Not yet."

"Good luck. Are you planning to publish it under your own name?"

Bart straightened. "What?"

"I know it sounds strange, but … it's not just *your* name. It's our name. It's Father's name. It's the name of this town."

A flush of heat came into Bart's face. "I know, but this is my work."

"I'm just saying, it's not just about you."

"James, it's not about any of us. I'm just trying to—"

"We know what you're trying to do."

Bart grabbed his old wooden desk chair, placed it at the side of his brother's bed, and sat. "Listen, I know how you feel. It hasn't been easy growing up and having to deal with a brother who popped out of the womb with different views. I know that all those years of discussions and debates and arguments between me and the two of you, especially Father, made life uncomfortable, even miserable at times, but that's in the past."

"So you write a book instead, by Bart Trask, agnostic-slash-atheist."

"Hey, come on, that's not fair."

"You're going to break his heart."

"James, I'm simply writing about Jesus. What you make of it—"

"You said there was something else new?"

Bart shifted in his chair. "Yes. I'm afraid this one's going to be tougher to tell you than the book."

James glanced at the open bedroom door, closed it, and returned to his bed. "What is it?"

Bart walked toward the window. He looked at the church and took a deep breath. "There's something I'd like to do. It means a great deal to me." He turned to James. "The reason I want to tell you is because ... well, I need your help."

"You need *my* help? That's a new one. You've never asked for my help once, ever, your entire life."

"I need you to help me with Father."

"With Father?" James frowned. "Are you feeling well?"

"I need his permission for something."

"Permission? For what?"

Bart returned to his chair. "I've begun to think about a series of lectures focusing on Jesus I'd like to take on the road and record for social media. I think if it's informative and entertaining, a general audience would be interested. I have a rough idea about what I'd like to say in both the book and on social media, but I feel in order to get it *right*, to present something of real value to the average person on the street, I need to be sure that I can address every imaginable question that may come my way. For that, my scholarship isn't enough."

Bart pushed himself forward in his chair. He locked onto his brother's eyes. "To help me with the book and lecture series, I feel I need to cut my teeth on a fully engaged audience of evangelicals who would be eager to challenge me, from *their* perspective, with tough questions, no holds barred, you know, give me a really hard time. The question is, where can I get that kind of audience? Then it hit me. Why not here, in Traskville?"

James sat bolt upright. His eyes widened. "What? Please don't tell me you want to use the church."

"No, of course not. Remember the old Stafford church, down the street?"

"That falling-down wreck?"

"Stafford says it's actually in pretty decent shape. He plans to renovate it and re-open the church in the fall. He's agreed to let me use it as a lecture hall for the next couple of months. I was thinking the lectures could run on Saturday afternoons through the spring and into the summer. I could come in on Friday evenings and go back on Sundays. The flight is only about an hour and a half."

"You want to give lectures undermining the divinity of Christ less than a mile down the street from Father's church? Have you lost your mind?"

"James, I have no intention of undermining—"

"Why here, right under our noses, in Traskville? It's a big country."

Bart stood. "I just told you, for the audience. I could probably fill a hall at UNC with a mix of liberal Christians, conservative evangelicals, and everybody else in between, but what could I hope to get out of them in that setting other than the usual polite academic pushback? I don't need polite academic pushback. I need uninhibited, heart and soul, fire and brimstone pushback." He pointed toward the window. "The people of Traskville, they *know* me. I'm the infamous lost son who finally came out as an agnostic, stopped going to church, and to the bewilderment of all, went off to the big city to get himself an education on the Bible and Jesus. The whole town of evangelicals is going to want to know what I have to say. As a Trask, I'm someone whose opinion *matters* to them. What better place to get the feedback I need than here?"

James glared at his brother. "Why the heck should the folks of Traskville be interested in what *you* have to say? They know you've abandoned the faith."

"Oh, they'll be interested. I've come back to talk about Jesus. If nothing else, morbid curiosity will fill the place to the creaky rafters."

"The second you open your mouth they'll be out for blood, or run you out of the place."

"Maybe, maybe not. I'll be challenged hard, that's for sure, but that's exactly what I need."

James walked over to the window. "If doing this down the street isn't bad enough, you have the gall to deliver this anti-Christian message in a church, of all places. Talk about false advertising...."

"James, it's not anti-Christian."

"You're just doing this to shake people's faith, to pull them away from God."

"I'm doing no such thing. I'm just a New Testament scholar talking about Jesus. That's all; nothing more."

"It's like Father and I have said to you before. You have no faith in Jesus because you're incapable of faith. For you, everything has to be *proven*." He shook his head. "I guess that's what your university teaches you."

"Hey, come on, that's not fair." Bart joined his brother at the window. "Look, I'll admit there are lots of people like that, but believe me, I'm not one of them. I happen to think faith plays an important role in life, but so does evidence."

James looked out at the church. "Yeah, right."

Bart gently placed his hand on James's shoulder. "If I were to ask people to have faith in Alpha-Beta, the God of the universe, would they, just like that, without any additional information? Of course not. Faith is important, but it doesn't exist in a vacuum. It's always based on something—information, evidence, call it what you like. There's no getting around it. This evidence, it's almost never proof, not even close, but it is the necessary springboard which makes the leap of faith possible. Since Christian faith is based on scripture, it only makes good sense to learn all we can about the text, in all the ways available to us. That's all I'm trying to do."

James pulled away. "You don't think we do that? You don't think devout Christians study the Bible? Father went to seminary. We've spent countless hours studying the Bible. You seem to think that university is the only place to learn anything, that you somehow have a monopoly on wisdom. Well, you're wrong."

"I'm not saying that at all." Bart sat on the wooden ledge just below the window. "Come on, James, you know me better than that. We've talked about this for years. I'm very well aware that lots of great scholarship has come from devout Christians studying the Bible from a religious point of view, as a holy book. All I'm saying is that there's another well-established way to study the Bible. I'm not saying it's a better way, I'm just saying it's a different way, a way that can teach us things about the life and times of Jesus that we may not get from a purely devotional perspective."

James scoffed.

"Hey, listen, I'm not going to say that my approach doesn't challenge the beliefs of the evangelical Christian. I think it does, but I have no interest in telling anyone, especially Christians, what to believe. What people make of it all is their business."

"So what do you want from Father?"

"His permission to give the lecture series. I know I don't need it but, well, it's a matter of respect. A year ago I may have bulldozed ahead with this, but not now." Bart rose to face his brother. "Look, I know how you feel about this, James, but I'm hoping you'll look past that and help me convince Father to at least give me his okay."

James returned to his bed and picked up his book. "I'm sorry, I can't do that."

Bart's shoulders sank. He returned to his chair. "Can I ask you why?"

James snapped his book shut. "You know why. For the very same reason you feel the need to ask for his permission in the first place. Because a Trask talking about Christ this way, especially right under Father's nose, would upset him deeply. He doesn't deserve that, especially from you, his son. If you care about him, you'll take your little dog and pony show elsewhere."

Bart straightened. His face flushed. "Dog and pony show?"

"I'm sorry. I can't help you."

For a moment, Bart looked directly into his brother's eyes, then lowered his head and nodded. "I understand," he said softly. "Thanks for hearing me out."

"Are you still going to ask him?"

"Yes."

"You're going to anger him. You're going to break his heart."

Bart looked away. "I hope not."

"Can you at least wait until after the party tomorrow?"

"Yes, of course."

With a loud exhale and a shake of his head, James got up and left the room, slamming the door behind him.

The following morning, Bart rolled over in bed and checked his phone. Six-fifteen. The ceiling, the walls, the furniture, his brother still sleeping in the double bed across the room in the pre-dawn Saturday morning, the smell in the bedroom.... Everything was the very same as it had always been years ago when they were children, and then teenagers, and then, finally, young adults. Even the sheets felt and smelled the same.

He thought of his girlfriend, Sarah. She'd be arriving at eleven to finally meet the family. He couldn't wait to see her sweet face and show her around. He crept over to James's bed and firmly nudged him. "Good morning, brother."

James rolled over. "What time is it?"

"Time for breakfast."

"It's still dark."

"Not for long."

"Go away."

After a long hot shower and a perusal of his emails, Bart descended the stairs. He found his parents at the kitchen table, the same round oak table at which he had surely taken his first meal. For a moment he saw his infant self in the wooden highchair, baby food covering much of his face, sitting right

12

next to his beaming young mother. Bart glanced at the food—biscuits and white gravy, sweet milk waffles, fluffy scrambled eggs, country ham, fried potatoes, orange juice, and coffee. He smiled.

"Good morning, folks. Happy anniversary."

Theodosius reached for the ham. "Good morning."

Bart's mother smiled. "It's so nice to have both boys home."

Bart filled his plate. "Excited about the party?"

Linda squeezed her son's arm. "We are. We're glad you're both here to share it with us. How are things in Chapel Hill?"

"Great. It feels really good to finally have tenure."

Theodosius shook his head. "I still can't believe that teachers in the Department of Religious Studies could be agnostic. You're teaching religion!"

Linda turned to her husband. "Now Theo," she said with a hint of gentle reproach, "you know the rules. No talk of religion at the table."

"Father, it's not a seminary, it's a state-funded university. I'm a New Testament scholar. My personal beliefs—"

"People who don't have the faith shouldn't be lecturing on the Bible. I think it's—"

Linda smacked her spoon on the table and glared at her husband. "Enough!" She turned to her son and smiled. "We're so excited to meet Sarah," she said, her voice suddenly loving.

Bart glanced at his mother and grinned. He'd seen this before. "I'm glad. She should be here by lunch."

"Well, that's just fine. If you don't mind me asking, how serious are you two?"

Bart smiled. "She's the one."

"Oh, that's wonderful. Please tell us all about her."

"She's a great gal, and a smart cookie. She's completing her PhD in evolutionary psychology."

James entered the kitchen with sleep in his eyes, his hair a mess, and his housecoat open. "Good morning."

His father smiled. "Good morning, James. Have a seat."

Linda chuckled. "Now all we need is Junia and little Thomas, and we'd all be back together."

Bart filled his brother's coffee cup. "I can't wait to see them."

Linda laughed. "Oh, the little guy. He's as cute as ever, running around the house like a holy terror."

Theodosius pushed his empty plate away and turned back to Bart. "Where is she from, your Sarah?"

"Upstate New York."

"Where did you meet her?"

"At one of my lectures, in a synagogue."

A conspicuous silence suddenly filled the room, amplifying the sounds of clanging knives and forks, the tick of the grandfather clock, the chirp of a bird outside, even the sound of chewing.

Linda refilled her husband's coffee cup. "Theo, isn't it great to have the boys together at the table?"

"Yes, Mother." He wiped his mouth and stood. "Excuse me. I've got some work to do."

After helping to clean up the kitchen, James and Bart walked out onto the veranda.

James looked up at the sky. "You had to mention the synagogue."

"Oh, come on, James. Really?"

"I just thought you'd...."

"I'd what, avoid all things that might ruffle his feathers? Is that what it's like around here? Everybody on high alert? He asked me a question. I answered it. What would you rather I do, tell him I met her at a Bible study? I can't help it if he doesn't approve of—"

"He's not anti-Semitic, you know."

"I know he's not."

James pushed the back of his father's favorite rocking chair, sending it swinging. "Remember that tornado last year outside of Montgomery that nearly wiped out a small neighborhood, including a synagogue? Guess who was out at the destroyed synagogue giving out food baskets and helping with the clean-up? And not a word about Jesus."

"I know. Junia told me." Bart grabbed the back of the rocking chair, abruptly arresting its motion. "Look, I know he's a good man, with a good heart. He lives his faith. I know all that. I just wish he'd ... let it go, let *me* go, you know, accept who I am."

"Not while you're his son."

Bart stared at the swing hanging from the massive oak. "Remember when we used to play on that thing, for days at a time? We had so much fun."

James flashed a brief smile and nodded. "We sure did."

"Tell me, do you miss those days?"

James shrugged. "I don't know. I guess so." He headed for the door. "I'll talk to you later."

The screen door snapped shut, leaving Bart alone with the swing and thoughts of childhood.

From the cozy confines of his favorite rocking chair on the veranda, Bart spotted Sarah pull into the driveway. He sprinted down the three wooden steps, threw open the door to her rental SUV, glanced at her newly purchased light-blue sun dress hugging her slender frame, and smiled. "Welcome, sweetheart."

Sarah emerged from the vehicle with her characteristic smooth grace, a natural balletic-like fluidity of motion. She wrapped her bare arms around his neck, pulled him toward her, and lightly kissed him on the lips. "Are you doing okay, sweetheart?"

Bart took a half step back, gently grasped her delicate hands, and locked onto her large brown eyes, half hidden by strands of wavy jet-black hair blowing in the breeze. For a moment, the weight of his concerns evaporated. "I'm glad you're here. Come on in. Mom can't wait to meet you."

"What about your father?"

"Him too." He escorted her into the house.

Linda greeted Sarah with a warm smile and a hug. "Welcome to our home. I'm so glad you could join us."

"I'm glad to be here. Bart has told me all about you and the family."

James appeared from the kitchen. "You must be Sarah."

"And you must be James. I'm pleased to finally meet you."

"Likewise."

Linda looked toward the staircase. "James, go get your father. He's still upstairs fretting over tomorrow morning's sermon."

"The sermon I wrote?"

"The very same, or what's left of it. You know him."

Theodosius descended the stairs. Bart placed his hand behind his girlfriend's back. "Father, I'd like you to meet Sarah."

He approached her, extended his hand, and offered her a polite smile. "I'm Pastor Trask. Welcome to our home."

"Thank you. Happy anniversary. I'm glad to be part of the celebrations."

After a few minutes of light conversation about the weather and the trip down from Chapel Hill, Linda escorted the family to the dining room table for lunch. Bart filled bowls with their mother's tomato barley soup while James brought in sandwiches. Before eating, James, Linda, and Theodosius bowed their heads. After a moment's hesitation, Sarah also bowed her head, closed her eyes, and became still.

As James quietly recited a brief offer of thanks, Bart flashed back to a conversation he'd had with Sarah several weeks earlier over coffee at his apartment in Chapel Hill.

"I see," she had said. "Would it be okay to join in when they bow their heads?"

Bart shrugged. "Sure, if you'd like."

"What do *you* do?"

"I usually bow my head and close my eyes."

"What do you think of when your eyes are closed?"

Bart crossed his arms and tugged at his right earlobe, a curious habit he had fallen into years ago whenever faced with a deep "think." He shrugged. "I don't know. I feel compelled to give thanks, but . . . to whom, or what? I usually come up with something—my parents, friends, all those who have come before me paving my way, the cosmos—but I've got to say, nothing ever seems to feel completely satisfactory. It's not that I'm ungrateful for my life. It's just...."

"Luck."

"What?"

"It's all those things you said, but it's also luck. The fact that you have decent food, a hot shower, and a comfortable bed, among other things, makes you luckier than most."

"So that's what it's all about, huh, gratitude and luck?"

She laughed. "Something like that."

Bart snapped back to the present. As if in unison, all eyes opened, heads lifted, and lunch began.

Linda turned to Sarah. "I hear you work with Bart at the university. What do you do?"

"I'm finishing up my studies."

"What are you studying? Bart mentioned something about psychology, I think."

"I'm studying an ancient society in Israel, how they survived in tough times."

"I see," Linda said vaguely.

"I was born in Tel Aviv and lived there until I was twelve, so I have a deep connection with the land and the people."

"Do you ... um, attend a synagogue?"

Sarah smiled kindly. "No, I'm not religious."

Linda glanced at Bart. "If you don't mind me asking, what does your family think of that?"

Sarah frowned. "That I'm not religious?"

Linda nodded. "Yes. I'm sorry, if that's too personal...."

"No, not at all. My parents are fine with it. They lost their faith after most of their family—my grandparents and so on—were exterminated by the Nazis."

Linda gently lowered her spoon into her soup and looked at Sarah. "I'm so sorry."

Sarah forced a smile. "It's okay. It's good to say it out loud once in a while."

James frowned. "Why, if I may ask?"

"I don't really know. I mean, it's hard to describe. Maybe by remembering, by not running away from it, it reminds me what terrible things are still possible if we don't pay attention."

Theodosius coughed. "And turn to our Lord God."

Linda firmly gripped her husband's forearm, turned to Sarah, and smiled. "Well, we're happy you're here to join us."

Bart directed the conversation to a host of lighter things, including a brief history of his parents. After lunch, James and Theodosius disappeared to finalize the Sunday sermon. Linda glanced at the grandfather clock. "My, how the time flies."

Sarah began stacking the empty soup bowls. "Can I help with party preparations?"

"No, it's all done. Anyway, it's mostly potluck. Nothing fancy. Go on, the two of you. Scoot. I'm going to go for a quick lie-down."

Sarah and Bart sat on the veranda steps. "Your mother, she's quite the woman."

"She sure is."

"You know, I kind of like your father, too."

Bart turned to her. "You do?"

"Sure. Why wouldn't I?"

"Well, at times he can be a little heavy-handed with his evangelism, like that comment about turning to God after you'd said you weren't religious."

Sarah rested her head on Bart's shoulder. "Don't be silly. He's just trying to take care of me, that's all. Are you getting anxious about asking him?"

Bart took a deep breath. "You could say that."

"I can imagine, especially after talking to James." She paused. "You know, I'm glad you're anxious about it."

"Why?"

Sarah caressed his arm. "Because it shows that you love him. You've got your passion and convictions, but you don't want to hurt him."

"But I am going to hurt him."

"You might be surprised."

"You don't know my father."

Sarah stood and turned to him. "I know it's going to be one hell of a tough conversation, but even if he says no, something good could still come out of it."

"Like the guy who survived the tsunami and said at least he was clean?"

Sarah laughed. "Something like that." She pointed to the old wooden swing next to the driveway. "Come on, let's go for a spin."

At three o'clock a large number of guests, by Bart's estimation about forty, arrived. Had they all come together in one big bus? Bart, Sarah, and Junia sat at one of seven large round tables set up on the freshly mown grass in the spacious side yard between the house and the church. Fluffy white clouds filled the late afternoon sky, providing intermittent respite from the unusually warm spring day. The forecast, suggesting possible showers, had prompted the erection of a large tent under which food and guests would be protected, if necessary.

Sipping on his ice-cold lemonade and wishing it were an ice-cold beer, Bart watched the guests greet his parents with shouts of joy, handshakes, hugs, and back-slapping. As he began to mingle with the guests, he found himself pleasantly surprised by the reception he received. Were they just being polite? After all, ten years earlier, he hadn't left under the best circumstances with many of these same people, who saw him, a Trask, as turning his back on not only the faith, but his father, their leader.

Sarah, wearing an attractive light-pink dress and just a hint of perfume, squeezed Bart's hand. "I'm having a great time."

Bart kissed her on the neck. "You smell delicious."

She pulled away slightly. "I'm sure we've got eyes on us."

"I hope so," he said, kissing her again.

"Behave," she said sternly. "Remember where you are."

Linda joined them. "Hello again. Are you enjoying yourselves?"

Sarah smiled warmly. "We are."

James emerged from the crowd. "Mom, shall we get the food out?"

"Yes please."

Sarah stood. "Can I help?"

Linda wrapped her arm around Sarah's shoulder. "That would be wonderful."

James pulled Bart aside. "Listen, we're going to have some speeches later. Do you want to get up and say something?"

"Sure. When?"

"During the meal. Sorry I didn't give you an earlier heads-up. If you'd rather not...."

"No, no, I'd like to say something."

James smiled. "Good. Come on, let's get the food out."

—⁓—

As Bart pretended to listen to the other speakers, he began to pull some thoughts together. After what felt like an interminable series of anecdotal musings from almost everybody present mixed with laughter and applause, James took the podium. His carefully prepared speech, which sounded a little like a Sunday sermon, was met with robust applause.

"And now, my long-lost brother, Bartholomew, would like to say a few words."

Restrained applause mixed with scattered murmurs filled the air. Bart jumped up and sprinted to the podium. He thanked his brother and looked out over the audience.

"Thank you all so very much for coming to our home, on this day of celebration." He paused. "I say 'our home' with fondness because although I've been away in Chapel Hill for a while, this is still my home. It will always be my home. I may have moved on, but I'll always cherish this place." He looked at his parents. "With all the great stories we've just heard, it's clear that you're both deeply loved by the whole town, this town we call Traskville. That's such a great thing to see, and not surprising. I could add many of my own stories, of course, but I'd really just like to say, in front of all these people ... I'd like to just thank you for being such great parents to us. Happy anniversary. I love you both very much."

Bart gave his mother a hug. He turned to his father. Theodosius stood, nodded, offered a brief smile, and extended his hand. Bart shook the hand and gave his father a hug. He returned to his seat amid polite applause and kissed Sarah on the cheek.

"Great job, honey."

Shortly following dessert, the gathering quickly broke up. Within minutes, nearly everybody had left. Bart and Sarah joined his parents, James, and Junia at the head table.

Linda shook her husband's forearm. "So what do you think, Father? Did you have fun?"

Theodosius smiled. "I most certainly did, Mother. I think everybody did."

"It's so nice to have the whole family back together." She turned to Bart. "When will you be going back, son?"

Bart glanced at Sarah and shifted in his seat. "We thought we might stay a few days, if that's okay."

Theodosius turned to Sarah. "I'd like to invite you both to attend Church Service in the morning."

Sarah smiled. "Thank you. We'll be there."

"Excellent. I look forward to hearing your thoughts on tomorrow's sermon."

"I look forward to sharing them with you."

Bart cleared his throat. "Father, I was wondering, would you be free for a few minutes tomorrow? There are a couple of things I'd like to discuss with you."

"Can it wait until after the service?"

"Yes, of course."

After several minutes of light conversation about a few of the guests, followed by a brief period of silence, Linda stood. "I hate to break this up, but there is a little more cleanup."

Sarah jumped up. "Leave it to us. You shouldn't have to clean up after your own party."

Later that evening, Bart and Sarah found themselves at a bar enjoying a cold beer. He squeezed her hand and smiled.

"Thanks for being here."

"I'm glad to be here. I'm enjoying myself."

"I'm sorry about my father's subtle evangelizing."

"What? The invite to church?"

"With discussion to follow."

She laughed. "He is a crafty one."

"You know he's going to try to convert you."

"As he should, in accordance with his faith. I'd be offended if he didn't."

"Really? Why?"

"It's like I said earlier. It means he's trying to look out for me, in his own sweet way. I like that. It's not just what people do that matters, it's why they do it."

Bart smiled wistfully. "It's funny. The way he looked at you…. He used to look at me that way too, before he gave up on me. I'm not saying I want those days back. I don't. It's just, well…."

"Oh, he loves you, as much as any father has ever loved a son. Under all that occasional pseudo-gruffness, I can tell. I know these things. It's just, well, he sees you as kind of a lost cause, when it comes to the faith."

"What are you going to say to him about the sermon?"

"Nothing that will upset him."

Bart lowered his head. "That'll be my job tomorrow."

"I'm surprised you brought it up at the table; I mean, about speaking to him."

"Yeah, well, I was surprised too, but when he said he wanted to talk to you, I figured I should get on with it."

"You want me there?"

"Yes … and no." He shook his head. "No, I suppose not."

"You still worried?"

He took a long sip of beer, finishing the bottle. "He can smell bad news a mile away, especially coming from me. I wish I hadn't said anything. He's probably lying in bed thinking about it."

"Don't worry, it'll be okay, no matter what happens."

Bart smiled. "You really believe that, don't you?"

"I do."

"Because it's coming from you, I'm going to believe it too. At least I'm going to try."

"That's all you can ask of yourself."

Bart kissed her on the cheek. "You know, I've got to say, I'm just so happy to be with you."

She grinned. "Right back at you, sweet man."

"I guess you could say I'm kind of lucky, huh?"

Sarah laughed. "You're damned right you're lucky, and don't forget it."

As dawn gave way to the promise of a new day, a razor-thin sliver of sunlight streamed into the siblings' bedroom, landing directly on the head of Bart's bed through a small gap in the blinds. For years this had served as Bart's wake-up call. Given James's inclination to sleep-in and his aversion to direct sunlight, his bed had been placed on the opposite side of the room, away from this brilliant early morning photon arrow. Bart looked up at the misshapen blinds, unchanged after all these years, glanced at his brother, and smiled. What fun they had growing up: fighting over the television, where to sit in the car, and all that other life-and-death stuff, long before they began to wonder about what happens after you die.

He crept down the hall, slipped into Sarah's room, threw off his pajamas, crawled into the double bed, and wrapped his arms around her naked body.

She squeezed his arm. "What took you so long?" she whispered.

He kissed her on the back of the neck. "We're going to have to be quick. I've got to get back before anybody wakes up."

She rolled over and pulled him onto her. Her delicate

warm hands found the small of his back. She shifted ever so slightly under him and whimpered.

"Quiet," he whispered.

She closed her eyes and threw back her head.

Several minutes later Bart was back in bed. James hadn't stirred.

An hour later, Sarah and Bart joined his parents for breakfast. As cereal was poured, eggs were eaten, and pancakes were passed around the table, Bart once again began to feel the weight of his upcoming conversation with his father. For a moment he considered bringing it up right then, but he caught himself. Not before Sunday Service, and not with Sarah and his mother present.

———∽∽∽———

They entered the church, Sarah a few steps ahead of Bart. A familiar face played familiar hymns on the organ, an old Hammond B-3 behind and to the right of the beautiful oak pulpit. The rising sun blazed through the large rectangular windows to their right, landing on the rows of old wooden pews to their left. The church, holding 260 worshippers, was nearly full. Bart spotted an empty row toward the back-right corner, but Sarah had already scooted ahead. Before he could catch up with her, she had slid into the sixth row next to the town pharmacist, a tall, thin, late middle-aged man with a narrow face and enormous eyebrows. Bart had known Joseph Pincer and his wife Winnie, who played the church organ, since Bart was a child. Bart pulled in next to Sarah just as another couple, also well known to him, the Alexanders, slid in next to him. Mr. Alexander, who had not attended the anniversary celebration, turned to his wife, pointed to Bart, and nodded.

As ten o'clock approached, the organ played a little louder, and the final stragglers filled the remaining empty seats. Bart looked around—the packed house, the music, the sun streaming in, all just as it was for all those Sundays when growing up. Since leaving for Chapel Hill, out of respect for his father, he had continued to attend church service when in town, so the experience had not lost its familiarity, but this time with Sarah at his side, it felt different. Was this her first time in a church?

Pastor Theodosius Trask, in his usual dark blue suit—the same one he'd worn for years—stepped up to the pulpit.

May God be with you all….

As Bart watched his father speak, he marveled, as he had done many times before, over the remarkable transformation from the man at home, whom his wife would call Theo and his children would call Father, to the pastor. To be sure, when away from the church his father would not infrequently carry an air of seriousness, of quiet authority—sometimes to extreme—until Mom would slap it out of him with a look, but at home he showed nothing like the powerful authority he exuded from the pulpit. To think, Bart mused, this powerful religious leader, whom the townspeople held in such high esteem, shaved in his underwear, regretted getting upset over trivial matters, had various minor aches and pains, laughed, and yes, on rare occasions, even cried. Bart was glad he knew that side of his father. Despite their marked difference of opinion, he respected, even admired the pastor, but he loved the man.

The sermon caught Bart's attention. The major theme revolved around the importance and responsibility of the

Christian to invite those outside the faith into the kingdom of God. Bart couldn't help but smile.

That son of a gun.

Bart whispered in Sarah's ear, "He's talking to you."

She smiled. "I know. Isn't that nice?"

Bart rolled his eyes.

They met Theodosius on the church steps on the way out. He smiled at Sarah. "Thank you for coming."

"Thank *you*. I enjoyed it."

"God has a loving heart for all his people."

Bart stepped forward, slightly between them. "Father, I was wondering when we could chat."

Theodosius glanced at his watch. "I need to be going into town. I should be back at two. We can talk then." He turned to Sarah. "Don't forget, I'd like to hear your thoughts on the sermon."

Sarah smiled. "Sure thing."

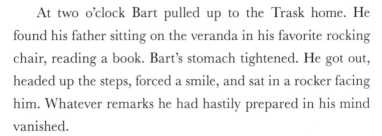

At two o'clock Bart pulled up to the Trask home. He found his father sitting on the veranda in his favorite rocking chair, reading a book. Bart's stomach tightened. He got out, headed up the steps, forced a smile, and sat in a rocker facing him. Whatever remarks he had hastily prepared in his mind vanished.

Theodosius looked toward Bart's car and frowned. "No Sarah?"

"She stayed back with Junia to help out with little Thomas."

"I'm curious to hear what she thought of the service."

For an instant, Bart considered teasing his father about the sermon but suppressed it.

"She's eager to talk to you about it."

"So what's on your mind?"

Bart's contentious conversation with James suddenly sprang back to life, tightening his jaw. He pushed it away. "I have a request."

"Go ahead."

Bart crossed his arms and tugged at his right ear.

"Bartholomew, what is it?"

"Before I get to that, I need to tell you a couple of things."

"I'm listening."

"I'm planning to write a book. It's about how Jesus came to be known as God by his followers."

Theodosius stopped rocking.

"It's for a general audience. The topic is well covered in academic circles but hardly at all for the average person. I thought it was time—"

"To tear down the divinity of Christ?"

Bart sat up. He knew this was coming, but it still stung him. "No, not at all."

Theodosius shook his head. "You just don't get it, do you?"

"Get what?"

"The Bible is not just any other text. It's a holy book. It has to be seen and interpreted as a holy book. If it is to be studied, it must be studied as a holy book, not just like any piece of history, bound by the laws of nature. You're trying to peel an apple as if it were an orange. It's all wrong."

"Father, I don't object to studying it as a holy book. I just think—"

"You said you had a request."

Bart took a deep breath. "I plan to start working on a series of lectures for the general public on Jesus, record them, and upload them to social media."

Theodosius looked away. "That should increase book sales."

"That's not why I'm doing it."

"So what's the request?"

Bart flashed back to James's response. "As part of my preparation for the book and lecture series, I want to get as much feedback as possible from Christians, especially conservative evangelicals. For the lecture series, I want to engage the audience with a robust Q and A session. Before going live I want to make sure I'm fully prepared for whatever might come my way on stage." A gust of wind blew across the veranda sending a low-hanging flower basket of spotted geraniums next to them dancing in the breeze. Bart welcomed the momentary distraction. "I believe the best way to prepare is to run a series of test lectures before a large, fully engaged audience who would be eager to hear what I have to say and challenge me hard on my views. But where could I find such an audience? Then it hit me. Why not right here, in Traskville?"

Theodosius sprang off the rocker, sending it flying backward, frightening off a group of birds perched in the massive oak. He jabbed his finger in his son's face, nearly touching his nose. "Stop right there! If you think for a second that I'm going to let you bring that ... secular flim-flam into my church, well you've gone and lost your mind."

The outburst pushed Bart back in his chair. "I didn't say

I wanted to bring it into your church. Please, if you'll just sit down and let me continue…."

Bart waited. A moment later, Theodosius dropped back into his rocker with a scowl. "Start talking."

Bart pushed himself to the edge of his rocker. "Remember the old Stafford church? I gave Pastor Stafford a call. He's agreed to let me have it on Saturdays for the next couple of months while it undergoes some minor renovations before he reopens it in the fall. It's perfect. I could deliver my lectures to the ideal test-audience, the townsfolk of Traskville."

"You can't be serious."

"I am serious. There's just one thing I'm going to need, before I proceed."

"I can't believe I'm hearing this."

"Your permission."

"My permission?"

"To be honest, in the past I may have just gone ahead without asking you, but as much as I want this, and believe me, I want it bad, I know in my heart doing that would be wrong. We've had our rough times, but you're still my father. I owe you that respect. So I'm asking you, from the bottom of my heart, can I have your permission?"

Theodosius looked away. His eyes narrowed.

"Father, please, I'm asking you—"

"I don't understand why you can't do this elsewhere. With your connections at the university, it should be easy to bring together a large group of evangelical Christians to give you the 'challenge' you claim you need."

"I could get a mix of Christians together, and it's likely the evangelicals would give me some polite feedback, but it just wouldn't be the same." He looked over at the church. "Father, the people of Traskville know me and my story: lifetime agnostic Bart Trask, son of Pastor Theodosius Trask, no less, goes off to study Jesus and now comes home to talk about him. They're definitely going to want to know what I have to say. Most of all, when they hear me, they're going to be especially eager to challenge me in every way possible. That's the good stuff; that's what I feel I need. There's only one place I can get that—right here, in Traskville."

"Maybe, but I think there's more to it than that."

"What do you mean?"

Theodosius smirked, the very same smirk Bart had seen many times before. "Oh, I don't doubt that you want to be challenged, but I know you, as well as I know myself. That's not all you want. You want to challenge *me*, and all the folks who call me Pastor Theo, don't you? We may have called a truce, but you still have this ax to grind with me. What better way than to talk to the very same people on Saturday who I talk to on Sunday."

"You think I'm trying to ambush you?"

"Call it what you like. It's nothing less than a slap in my face."

Bart ran his fingers through his hair and exhaled. "Father, I know it may feel that way, but that's not my intention, and that's not how people will see it. I'm simply asking you to let me be myself, do my thing, be who I really am. I've come to accept who you are and what you do. I even admire it, in a way. I'm just asking for the same from you."

"I see. So tell me, who are you?"

Bart rose, walked to the corner of the veranda, and sat on

the handrail. "Who am I?" He rubbed his eyes and looked over at the swing. "I suppose you can say I'm my own man, with my own ideas about what it is to be a human being and live in this world."

"You can say that again."

"But I'm also my father's son. I know you must feel that this apple fell far from the tree and then rolled all the way down the hill, but it's not true. I've been thinking a lot about that recently. It's funny. After years of feeling so different from you, I've begun to see how alike we really are."

Theodosius raised his eyebrows. "This I've got to hear."

"Our passion. The fire in our bellies for life, our work, what we believe…. Look at us. Up until recently, we've been at it for what, twenty years? I know it got us a little bit cranky at times, but deep down inside I don't think I'm wrong when I say that, in a strange kind of way, we both loved it. Now tell me, where did I get all that?"

Theodosius began rocking, showing no expression.

"I'll go one step further. If I'm here, wanting so badly to do this, it's *because* of you."

"Oh, so now it's my fault."

Bart jumped off the handrail. "Father, it's not a 'fault' thing."

"Then what are you saying?"

Bart returned to his rocker. "Look, we both know I never much cared for church service, but your sermons, now that was a different story. I loved them, not for the religious teaching, but for how and why you reached out to the people." Bart stopped rocking. He found his father's eyes. "Your passion, your command of language, your presence, your fervent desire to help people the best way you knew how. It dazzled me. I remember watching you, Sunday after Sunday, for as long as I can remember, not usually agreeing with your religious message but nevertheless feeling amazed, in awe of you. I remember one fine day thinking how marvelous this was, connecting with people in such a beautiful way, for no other reason than to try to help them. When I saw that, I knew that was for me, a thing I would want to do. I know it sounds crazy, but I think your sermons inspired me to become a professor. But not just any kind of professor. Someone who came out of the ivory tower and connected with the average person on the street the way you did, and still do, because you care. That's why I want to write my book, and that's why I want to do the lectures and the social media."

Theodosius rose, walked to the railing, and looked up into the oak tree. "I … I never knew you felt that way about my sermons."

"I never told you. I was too busy disagreeing with you."

The pastor smiled sadly. "How the church could have used you."

Bart stood next to his father. "It just didn't happen for me."

"If I say no, what then?"

"I'll understand."

"And then?"

"I'll take it somewhere else, probably to UNC. It won't be nearly as helpful to me as talking to the people I grew up with, but I'll make it work."

"You know, you've never asked my permission for anything."

"I think you're right. I wonder where I got that from?"

Theodosius walked off the veranda and sat on the swing. Bart's phone rang—Sarah. He shut off the phone and joined his father. They sat, silent and still. Bart would wait, all afternoon and into the evening if he had to, for an answer. If that answer was no, he was prepared to accept it.

Ten minutes later, Theodosius turned to his son. "I am to be given time, as much as I feel I need, to give a response to the group after each lecture. I must also take part in each Q and A session, until every single question is answered."

Bart caught his breath. For a moment, he couldn't speak. He jumped off the swing. "Yes, of course. Whatever you want. You got it. Would you like an outline of the lectures? I'm sure I could throw something together for you."

"No need; I already know what you're going to say."

"Father, thank you so much. I know this can't be easy."

"We'll see how you feel after we're done." Theodosius headed for the veranda. "Tell Sarah I'd still like to talk to her about today's sermon." He went into the house, leaving Bart standing next to the swing.

After a sound sleep, Bart pulled up to the old Stafford
Church with Junia and Sarah. A decrepit sign—a large
rectangle of decaying dark, weather-beaten wood hanging
from two uneven-length rusted chains supported by gray
rusted poles—greeted them at the road. From this makeshift
sorry mess they could make out a barely discernable few
words—*Holy Ground Church. Pastor Edmund Stafford.*

Bart looked at the little church, an unadorned, slightly
crooked, rectangular wooden structure with a short steeple
housing two small bells in the belfry—Bart had never heard
them ring—crowned with a conspicuously long, also slightly
crooked spire, broken off at the top. One could only imagine
the condition of the sanctuary.

They drove onto a narrow dirt road leading to a small
parking lot to the right of the church. Bart fumbled with his
keychain at the chipped and peeling wooden front door. The
handle almost came off in his hands. He pulled open the door
and cringed. The bottom hinge screeched loud enough to
wake the dead. They entered a tiny vestibule. The smell of
old wood and stagnant air hit his nose. Sheets of sunlit dust
danced in the foul air.

To Bart's surprise, the sanctuary seemed to be largely

intact except for cracks in four of the eight square windows high on the side walls. He inspected the eighteen rows of pews, separated by a narrow, slightly uneven center aisle. On a pew toward the front, he found an empty bottle of whiskey, bone dry and covered in dust, the label partially torn.

Sarah stood on the stage just behind the pulpit, half hidden by piles of boxes, broken furniture, and Christmas decorations. She pushed a few items aside. "Hey, there's a leak here. The wood floor is stained." She looked up. "I don't see a—wait, the roof is stained, kind of blotchy, just above me."

Junia joined her brother in the front row. "What happened to Stafford anyway?"

"I don't know. I think he was sick for a while."

"Looks like the place needs a lot of work. What do you want to do?"

"I'd like to put all this junk into the dumpster out back, so the contractors can get in here and do their thing."

"Isn't he kind of old to jump back into the church?"

"I'd say so, but, well, this place has been his entire life, you know?"

Sarah disappeared through a door at the back of the church. "Hey, come and see the living quarters."

They found themselves in a large rectangular room with a couch, chairs, and flat-screen TV with a cracked screen. They also discovered a kitchenette without appliances, a square wooden table and chairs, a tiny bedroom containing nothing but a heavily stained box spring leaning against the far wall, and an adjoining tiny bathroom with a shower.

A slight bulge in the carpet in front of the couch under a wooden coffee table caught Bart's eye. He peeled back the carpet, revealing a handle to a square trapdoor. Junia lifted the door, exposing a steep stone walkway of eight steps which led into a rectangular shaped room the size of a small bus with a cracked cement floor and stone walls. The height of the room just permitted Bart to stand erect. On the wall opposite the stairs, light streamed in from a square iron grate. Remnants of a window, now mostly missing, covered the grate. The room contained various items, including broken chairs, tables with missing legs, a ladder, old power tools, and boxes full of Bibles and hymnals. The place stank vaguely of animal excrement.

Returning to the church, they began their work, filling the dumpster, cleaning, and taking a careful inventory of all the repairs that would be needed—no electricity, dry toilets, leaky roof, broken windows, and front door issues.

Three hours later, they flopped onto the front pew, exhausted. The junk was gone, even from the basement, the entire church was swept, and all areas and items identified as needing repair were marked for the crews.

Bart rose. "I'll be back in a second." He returned with a cooler from which he produced a bottle of champagne and three plastic cups. He popped the cork. Champagne gushed over his hand and onto the floor. He filled the plastic cups and toasted their accomplishment.

The front door creaked open. James entered. Bart emptied his cup and poured a refill for all. "Look who the wind blew in."

James walked down the aisle, spotted the cork, picked it up, and handed it to his brother. "So now we're drinking alcohol in a church?"

Bart smiled. "Surprised to see you here."

"Can I have a word with you? It's about Father."

Junia glanced at Sarah. "We'll leave you guys alone."

They headed to the living quarters.

James looked around. "This place has seen better days."

Bart tossed the cork in the air and caught it. "It does need some work, but it should be just fine after some renovations."

"I asked Father about your conversation with him. I've got to say, I'm shocked he's doing this."

Bart sniffed the cork, squeezed it, and gave an approving nod. "I was a little shocked too, but there you go."

James averted his gaze and exhaled loudly. "You know, just because he gave you his permission doesn't mean he's happy about it."

"Oh, I know."

"I just wanted to say, it's not too late to take this somewhere else. It'll save you all this hassle."

Bart smiled. "Thanks, but I'm going to do it here."

"Don't you care how he feels?"

"Of course I do; that's why I asked him. I'm glad you're concerned about him, but don't worry, he can handle him-.self."

"I know he can, but he's already got so much on his plate with his busy schedule of community outreach in Birmingham."

"Hey, I think it's awesome you guys are working with Habitat for Humanity."

"He doesn't have enough time as it is. And now, this. He's going to spend hours working on this thing. You know how he is, preparing for his sermons."

Bart put his hands on his brother's shoulders and smiled. "Don't worry, he'll be just fine, okay? We'll be staying with Junia to give her a hand with little Thomas. That should help keep things quiet at home before the lecture."

James shook his head. "And to think, you were his favorite."

Bart frowned. "Favorite? Where did you hear that?"

"Please think about what I've said. It's not too late."

James left the church, slamming the screeching door behind him.

Bart joined Sarah and Junia at the kitchen table in the living quarters. He poured the few remaining drops of champagne into Sarah's cup.

Junia ran her finger over the label. "You know, I haven't had this in a while, not since—" She looked away, her eyes suddenly wet with tears. Sarah gently grasped her hand.

"Bart told you?"

Sarah nodded.

"A bad headache, and he was gone, just like that."

"I'm so sorry."

"We had just come back from our second anniversary party. We'd had so much fun." She caressed the neck of the bottle and flashed a mouth-only smile. "I actually just had a taste; I was three months pregnant." Her smile vanished. "When we got home he got a headache. I accused him of drinking too much. The headache got worse. He laid down. Ten minutes later, I went in to check on him." Tears rolled down her cheeks. "He was gone."

She tipped the bottle on its side. It rolled off the table, landing with a thud onto the uneven wooden floor, coming to rest in a corner. "The medical examiner called it an aneurysm. The doctor said he was born with it. Have you ever heard of such a thing? I can't believe it's been six years. A day doesn't go by I don't wonder ... why? I mean, why is a man, a good man, born with a death sentence?"

For a few moments, the three of them sat, staring with unfocused eyes at the middle of the table.

Junia stood. "I'm sorry, I didn't mean to get into all that. The champagne ... it all just came rushing back."

Bart retrieved the bottle, threw open the backdoor, and flung it into the dumpster. The bottle landed upright, resting on the pile of junk they had created. For a moment Junia stood staring at it, then bolted down the steps, snatched the bottle, sprinted back inside, slammed it down onto the center of the table, and turned to her brother. "I've already tried that. It doesn't work."

"What doesn't work?"

"You can't just throw away the past, as if it never happened. It's always there, around the corner, waiting to strike when you're not looking. I just wish I understood it better ... I mean the why."

"That's a tough one."

"Isn't that what you do? Try to understand the past?"

"Yeah, but what you're talking about, that's a different thing altogether, way above my pay grade."

Junia caressed the bottle. "Can I ask you a question?"

"Sure. I probably won't have an answer."

"This lecture series.... I think I understand why you're doing it. I even think I understand why you're doing it here. I just want to know one thing. I know how it's been between Father and you over the years. Please tell me you're not doing it to, you know, jab him."

"I'm not," he said softly.

"Are you sure? Because, I mean, it's not always easy to know things like this."

"I'm sure."

She nodded. "Okay. I just needed to hear it from you."

The three of them sat in silence at the table with the bottle between them. The sun began to set. The wind picked up, blowing the back door closed. Bart stood. "I think we've spent enough time in here for one day. Let's relieve Mom and go play with little Thomas."

Bart escorted Sarah and Junia out, leaving the champagne bottle on the table.

CHAPTER

The following morning Bart returned to the Church with Sarah to work on an outline for his lecture series. He placed a whiteboard on an easel in front of the communion table, dug a marker out of his pocket, and stared at the board.

"What's wrong, writer's block?"

"No. Quite the opposite. I want to say it all at once. It's a good thing I'm not a painter. I'd want to use all the colors in the same places. Wouldn't that be a pretty picture?"

"One idea at a time, sweetheart."

After an hour of scribbling while Sarah worked on her thesis, Bart capped the marker and rubbed his eyes. "I've had enough of this. You want to get some fresh air?"

"Sure. What did you have in mind?"

"I thought I'd get rid of the old sign and replace it with a nice new wood sign."

Sarah frowned. "You mean dig the holes, pour the cement...."

"Yeah, why not?"

She shrugged. "It seems like an awful lot of work. Are you worried Stafford won't cover it?"

"No. It's just ... I don't know, maybe it's just my way of

putting my personal stamp on the place. How does 'The Institute for the Study of Jesus' sound?"

"The *what?*"

"You don't like it?"

"It's just fine if you want to scare them off. 'Institute.' What the hell is that going to mean to these folks, except for some kind of fancy big-city building? And 'the study of Jesus.' Could you make it sound any more hoity-toity ivory tower? You may as well say PhDs only."

"Come on, isn't that a bit of an exaggeration?"

"No, I don't think so. You want to talk to the people in this town? Fine, just do it in a way they can understand."

"Sarah, they're not idiots."

"I'm not saying they're idiots. I'm just saying you've got to present it to them the right way. You get up there and start talking to the people like you're giving a PhD dissertation, and they'll run out the door as if the church were burning down. If you want to reach them, you're going to have to … I don't know … go campfire on them."

"Campfire?"

"Yeah. Pretend you're sitting around a blazing campfire roasting wieners with, say, three or four townsfolk, all interested to hear what you have to say."

"Wieners, huh?"

"Wieners, marshmallows, whatever. It's not just what you say, it's how you say it."

Bart chuckled. "I gotcha. Know your audience, right? Message received. Now can we get back to the sign? I'll need to go into town and get some supplies. The local hardware store should have all we need."

They returned an hour later. After pulling out the old sign, which required little more than a tap from his shovel, Bart began in earnest. Throwing his shovel into the black earth felt good under the warm, late afternoon sun. He flashed back to when he was a boy, when he and James cleared the backyard of rocks and tree stumps. How wonderful it had felt working under that same warm sun, unencumbered by deep thinking.

As Bart dug the holes and mixed the cement, Sarah assembled the frame of the sign, which consisted of sturdy wooden posts, and attached the square plywood board to the top post with hinges. They lowered the surprisingly heavy sign into the holes and poured the cement. After holding it in place for a few minutes, they gradually released their grip. Bart stood back and smiled. "Look at that, perfectly straight and even. We don't need no sign builders."

A gentle breeze came up, tipping over the sign. They looked at each other and laughed. Bart removed the plywood from the frame. "I guess we should have allowed the cement to harden before attaching this."

A few minutes later, with the help of some heavy string and stakes, they had the frame up and secured. Bart stood back to confirm proper placement. "That should do it. I'll attach the plywood later. How does the name—"

Out of the corner of his eye he caught a glimpse of a young woman walking toward them along the side of the road. As she passed them she quickened her pace and turned her head slightly away. She was tall and thin, no more than twenty, he figured. Her straight brown hair, parted in the middle, was cut above the shoulder, multiple strands hanging in her face.

She had grief in her eyes and a bruise under her left eye and cheek.

Bart caught up with her. "Excuse me, are you okay?"

She stopped abruptly, as if frightened, then passed him. "I'm fine," she said in a quavering voice.

He ran in front of her, causing her to stop. "I'm sorry, but you look like you may need some help."

She recoiled. "I said I'm fine. Let me go." Tears rolled down her cheeks.

Sarah joined them. "It looks like you've been beat up. What happened to you?"

She stared at Bart and frowned. "Bart? Bart Trask?"

Bart's eyes widened. "Jenn Adams?"

She wiped her eyes and nodded.

Bart turned to Sarah. "I used to babysit this young lady." He escorted her off the side of the road toward the sign. "This is Sarah, my girlfriend. Jenn, what happened?"

"It's nothing. I ... fell off my horse yesterday."

"Fell off your horse? Did you hurt anything else?"

"My back, a little. I'll be fine."

Bart noticed the large knapsack and looked down the road, lined by nothing but trees as far as the eye could see. "Where are you ... would you like a lift somewhere? I've got my car here."

She looked at the frame of the new sign and the church. "Are you a preacher, like your daddy?"

"No, I'm a teacher. I'll be using the church as a lecture hall. Is there somewhere I can drop you off?"

"Can you take me into town, to the bus station?"

"Is that where you were going? That's over two miles."

"I was hoping to get a ride, but I haven't seen a single car go by."

Bart glanced at Sarah. "Sure, I'll take you. Where are you off to, if you don't mind me asking?"

Jennifer averted her eyes. She slumped to the ground next to the sign and began to sob.

Bart touched her shoulder. "Listen, why don't you come inside the church for a minute? We've got some snacks and water. You can rest a while."

She shook her head. "No, I've got to go."

"What time is your bus?"

"I don't know."

"You don't know?" He kneeled beside her. "Listen, Jenn. Whatever you've got going on, I know it's none of our business, but we'd like to help you. Why don't you come on inside for a snack and a drink, and then I'll take you, okay?"

She slowly got to her feet. Bart caught a glimpse of a nasty bruise on her left forearm. He grabbed her knapsack. "Come on." She didn't budge. Bart waited. A few moments later, she took a deep breath, nodded, and followed them into the church.

With wide eyes she glanced at the pews, the podium, the massive wooden cross on the back wall, even the roof.

"Is it safe in here? I mean, it looks a little crooked."

Bart smiled. "It's safe."

"How long has it been empty?"

"A couple of years. The pastor plans to renovate and reopen it."

They entered the living quarters. Sarah pointed to the table. "Have a seat. Can we offer you a drink and something to eat?" From her own knapsack she retrieved three bottles of water and a box of granola bars and placed them on the table. "Help yourself."

Jennifer grabbed the water. "Thanks."

Bart pushed the box of granola bars toward her. "Apologies for the mess. We just got the place a few days ago."

Jennifer took a large gulp of water. "What lectures are you going to be giving?"

"I'll be talking about Jesus and the New Testament."

She frowned. "Why here? I mean why not at your daddy's church?"

"That's a bit of a long story." He paused. "That sure is a hell of a bruise on your face. You're lucky you weren't seriously injured, or even killed."

Jennifer lowered her head. Bart waited. She said nothing.

"How are your folks? I can remember seeing you guys at church way back in the day."

Fresh tears filled her eyes. She sprang up, bumping the table and sending the unopened bottle of water tumbling onto the floor. "I'm sorry. I've got to go."

Bart stood. "Jenn, what's wrong? What's going on?"

She shook her head. "Nothing. I've just … I've got to get out of here."

Sarah gently placed her hand on Jennifer's shoulder. She flinched. "Jennifer, what happened to you? Did you really fall off a horse?"

Jennifer headed for the door leading into the sanctuary. "Thank you for your kindness."

Sarah bolted for the door, blocking her departure. "Bart, can you please leave us alone for a few minutes?"

He hesitated, then went out the back door. As he headed around the side of the church to his car, Sarah's voice, filled with such a softness and tenderness as he had never heard from her, froze him under the kitchen window.

"It's okay, Jenn, you can tell me. You're safe here. What really happened to you? You didn't fall off a horse, did you?"

A few seconds later, Sarah's voice rang out. "What? Who did this to you? Your boyfriend?"

Bart waited, straining to hear the answer, but could hear nothing. He was about to leave when Sarah's question once again stopped him cold.

"Your *father*? Why?"

Bart stiffened. He pressed himself against the wooden slats below the window and held his breath.

"Why, Jenn? What happened?"

"He was drunk. He's always drunk. He said he wanted to teach me a lesson, to fix me."

"What lesson?"

"It doesn't matter. I just have to get away."

"It does matter! Why did he beat you up? Please tell me. We want to help you."

"He got angry and hit me because...." Her voice trailed off.

"A girlfriend? You mean...."

"Yes, I'm a lesbian, okay?"

Bart held quiet and still, waiting for more, but nothing came. After several minutes he ran to his car and jumped inside, a sheen of sweat covering his face, trying to organize his chaotic thoughts. Poor girl. She needed help, but what to do? He would wait until Sarah called him.

Twenty minutes later, the call came.

"Where are you?"

"I'm in my car."

"Come back in. We need to talk."

"I heard."

"What?"

"As I was going to my car, I happened to overhear part of your conversation. I'm sorry. I couldn't help but stop and listen."

"It's okay. Just come back. She desperately wants to leave, but I've convinced her to stay until you come back."

"Am I supposed to know?"

"I'll tell her. Hurry, before she disappears on us."

Bart entered the church, crept up to the entrance of the living quarters, and stood in the open doorway. The two women sat at the kitchen table. Jennifer sat back, head lowered, wisps of hair hanging limp in her face, staring with wet unfocused eyes into her hands. Sarah sat forward, her hands outstretched across the table, staring with tear-filled eyes at Jennifer. He slowly lowered himself into his chair between them. They sat in silence, broken only by the occasional creaking of the church and gust of wind.

Bart took a slow deep breath. "Jenn, I'm so very sorry about what happened."

"You're the only two people in this town who know. Sarah promised me you won't tell anybody."

"We won't. What we'd like to do is help you. What can we do? Do you want to go to the hospital, to get checked out? Maybe you should call the police."

"No! I mean, you've done so much already. I just need to get out of here."

"Where were you going? To see your girlfriend?"

Jennifer walked over to the back door and peered out the window. "I wish," she said softly.

Sarah approached her. "Does she know about this?"

"No. She's in the military. I couldn't reach her. She's stationed in Germany."

"What about your mother? Does she know?"

"Mom died three years ago. Cancer. That's when he started drinking more."

"I'm so sorry. Have you told anybody else about this?"

"No."

Bart joined them. "So, where were you going, Jenn?"

"Nowhere. Just ... away, so I can breathe again."

"Do you have any friends or family you can reach out to?"

"I've got cousins and a couple of aunts scattered all over the south, mostly in Tennessee and Georgia, but I haven't seen them since I was a little kid."

"What about friends?"

Jennifer shrugged. "Do you remember Amber? We were best friends growing up. I think you babysat both of us a couple of times." She smiled wistfully. "Remember how she loved to play jump rope?"

Bart grinned. "I sure do."

"We were together all the time. But then, well, she started chasing boys. She still lives at home, but I don't hardly ever see her. I heard she's engaged."

Sarah gently touched Jennifer's shoulder. "You don't think she'd be willing to help you?"

"How could she? Anyway, I think she suspected something about me. That's why she pulled away. It doesn't matter. As long as I have Tracy, everything will be fine."

Sarah turned back to the table. "Come, let's sit. We'd love to hear about her."

Jennifer snatched a granola bar out of the box on the table and devoured it in two bites. "About a year ago I met her at a party in Birmingham. It all went so fast. At the party there were a few lesbian couples. They were so open about it. I was shocked. When I saw them, all at once I felt this massive weight come off my back, a weight I've been carrying for so long I kind of forgot it was there. They asked me if I was a lesbian. Even from them, the question shocked me. I opened my mouth to speak, but I couldn't push out even a single word. My eyes got so watery I couldn't even see them. All I could do was nod."

Jennifer smiled. "They were so sweet to me. I guess they could see I was struggling. Tracy was one of the girls in the group. We went for a walk. I went home that night with hope. We saw each other the next day. We've been together ever since, in secret, until she left three months ago. The plan was for me to wait for her and then leave this grubby little town to be with her."

Sarah dug three more bottles of water out of her bag and put them in the middle of the table. "What happened yesterday?"

"I accidentally left my phone on the kitchen table. He happened to see multiple posts from her. He saw a lot. When I walked into the kitchen and saw him with the phone in his hand, I almost passed out. He threw the phone down, smashing it. Then he came after me, drunk off his ass, as usual, and hit me. He said he didn't raise me that way, and Mom would be ashamed, and all terrible things like that." Fresh tears filled her eyes. "I ran into my room and locked the door. This morning, he was out cold, like he is every day until noon. That's when I decided to leave."

Bart glanced at his watch. "Do you have any money?"

"A little. This morning I emptied my bank account. Two hundred and fifty dollars."

"How far do you expect to go with that?"

"I don't know. I'll worry about that later." She pressed her lips together. Her big eyes glistened. She slowly rose. "I should get going." She grabbed her knapsack. Tears rolled down her cheeks. "I can't thank you enough, both of you, for everything you've done." She paused. "If that ride to the bus depot is still available, I'd sure appreciate it."

Bart glanced at Sarah. "Hang on; I've got an idea." He walked to the doorway into the church, peered into the sanctuary for a moment, then turned to her. "I'd like to make you an offer."

Jennifer shook her head. "I'm sorry, but you've done too much already. I really should go."

Bart motioned her back to the table. "Please hear me out, just for a minute."

Bart once again sat between the two women. He grasped Jennifer's hand. "Would you like to stay here, in the church, until Tracy returns?"

She frowned. "What? Here? No, I can't do that."

"Why not? After I get things set up and the renovations are complete, I'll be going back to Chapel Hill during the week for the summer. I'll only be here on the weekends, to give my presentations. Nobody will know you're here."

Jennifer stared at Bart, her mouth slightly open. "I ... I'll be discovered."

"No you won't. When I'm gone, you'll keep the doors locked." He pointed to the back door. "You've got ten acres of woods back there, with not a house in sight. The area just outside the door is mostly surrounded by a tall, thick hedge. Nobody in the world but us would know you're here. I'll stock the place to the rafters with supplies and see you every weekend."

"What about the pastor? Won't he be coming around to see his place?"

"Not until the fall. He's in California with his brother."

"What about the work crews? They'll see me."

"Yes, but they won't know you. They're all coming in from Birmingham. I'll check with the contractor to make sure none of the crew live around here."

"What about the people coming in to see your presentations?"

"Don't worry; nobody will be coming back here."

Her face contorted. "No, I really can't."

"Why not? Give me one good reason why not?"

She shrugged. "I ... I don't know. I can't pay you."

"Pay me?" He paused. "Actually, you can. First of all, I was going to have to keep an eye on the place from afar, but it would be great, especially after the renovations, if I had somebody to watch over it when I'm not here, you know, kind of like a security guard. Second, after the renovations are complete, I'll be getting a cleaning crew in, but they're probably not going to do a great job. The place is going to need a thorough cleaning, and perhaps a few last-minute touch-ups, to

make it presentable for an audience. I'm thinking you probably wouldn't really have to do much, but knowing you're here,
watching over the place, and helping to make it presentable,
all that would be a great help to me. I'll get you one of those
pay-as-you-go phones so you can secretly keep in touch with
me twenty-four-seven."

Jennifer shook her head. "I really don't know what to say."

"Say yes, you'll do it."

She crept toward the doorway leading into the sanctuary
and peered inside. "Are you sure it would be safe? I mean, I
wouldn't be discovered?"

Bart firmly squeezed Sarah's hand. "Absolutely. If anybody comes back for a minute or two, I'll let you know. You
can hide in the basement. Well, it's not really a basement; it's
more like a storage area. It's small, but it'll do just fine." He
pointed to the floor. "The stairs are right there, under the
coffee table. When nobody is in the church, which, as I say,
will be most of the time, you'll have the run of the place. As
you saw, the big windows are high above the floor, and there
are no other houses around here, so you'll be safe. What do
you think?"

Jennifer stood rigid, her slender shoulders hunched, her
disheveled hair hanging over her flushed face. "I ... I just
don't know."

"Come on, you've got to admit, it's a better option than
wandering around some strange town with no money."

"My father and a bunch of his buddies are going to come
looking for me. If they find me here, it won't go well for you."

"That's not going to happen. There's no way in the world
anyone is going to find you." Bart escorted her back to the

table. "Look, you're in trouble. You need help. You need a friend. We want to help you. While you're here, you can help me. I'm telling you, Jenn, if you could watch the place for me, clean it up, keep it clean, and take care of a few odds and ends, it would make my life a hell of a lot easier."

"Are you sure I'd be helping you?"

"Yes, I'm sure. Believe me, it would be one less thing for me to worry about. You'd be putting my mind at ease."

"I don't think I've ever put anybody's mind at ease."

"So, do we have a deal?"

She covered her face in her hands and wept. Bart gently placed his hand on her shoulder and waited. A few moments later, she nodded.

"Okay, then," he said softly. "Don't worry; we'll take care of you."

On the way to the car, Sarah stopped Bart. "Didn't you instruct the cleaning crew to give the place an especially good scrubbing after cleaning up the mess?"

"I did."

"You don't really *need* someone to watch over the place, clean up after the cleaning crew, or do odd jobs, do you?"

"No, not really."

Sarah squeezed his hand and smiled. "Come on, let's go get her some things."

Sarah and Bart returned with groceries, linens, toiletries, a mini fridge, a small microwave oven, an air mattress, some clothing, and a pre-paid cell phone. In their absence, Jennifer had managed to give some of the sanctuary and the living quarters a scrubbing. Without running water, a functioning toilet—a porta potty had been delivered for the workers— or electricity, her first night would be a little rough, but the electrician, plumber, and a work crew were all scheduled for the following day.

They sat at the table, picking at a bag of popcorn, sipping on warm beer, and saying little, the silence surrounding them broken only by the creak of the floor and wind in the trees. Sarah offered Jennifer a reassuring smile. "I'm afraid I've got to get going. Busy day tomorrow. Don't worry; we're going to get you through this, safe and sound, we promise."

Jennifer jumped up and hugged her, a tight, sustained hug. "Thank you, for everything."

"Thank you for letting us into your life. I'll see you soon."

Jennifer flopped back into the kitchen chair, buried her fingers in her hair, threw back her head, and closed her eyes. "I can't believe this is happening."

Bart pushed a beer toward her. "That makes two of us."

"I didn't think anybody around here would understand, let alone help me."

"Well, I'm glad we could prove you wrong."

"I remember when you used to come over and babysit me. You were so nice. And now look at you, all grown up, a fancy college professor. And look at me. I guess we went our separate ways, huh?"

"I suppose, but you know, you and me, I'd say we've got a lot in common."

Jennifer chuckled. "That's a laugh. I'm nothing like you."

"You may be surprised. As a lesbian woman growing up here, in Traskville, you don't exactly fit in, do you?"

"I don't feel like I fit in, that's for sure."

"Well, in a way, me too. You see, I'm not at all religious."

Jennifer's eyes widened. "You're not?"

"Nope."

"You know, now that you mention it … my father did say something about you years ago, how you were the black sheep, or something like that. It didn't mean much to me at the time."

"What does it mean to you now?"

"Well, it does seem kind of strange. You are your daddy's son, aren't you?"

Bart grinned. "I certainly am."

"But you said you were going to preach about Jesus."

"I didn't say preach. I'm a professor. I take a different approach."

Jennifer frowned. "Different than your daddy? Why would you do that?"

"You're just going to have to listen to my lecture to find out, won't you? You'll be able to hear it from here, in secret."

"If you're not a believer, why are you even talking about him?"

Bart shrugged. "A whole bunch of reasons. He's one of the most important people who ever lived. He changed the world. Besides, he fascinates me."

"Does your daddy know? I mean, that you're not a believer?"

"He sure does."

"Wow. That must be something."

"You could say that."

Jennifer glanced at the small, plain wooden cross hanging over the television. "Yeah, well, I can think of another thing we've got in common. We're both going to Hell."

"You really believe that?"

She took a long sip of beer. "That's what your daddy thinks."

"Do *you* believe it?"

She lowered her head. "I don't know. I don't want to believe it. Tracy doesn't believe it."

"Neither did Jesus."

Jennifer's head shot up. "What? What do you mean?"

"I know it sounds strange, but these modern notions of Heaven and Hell that we have, you can't find them in the Bible. They didn't even exist during the life of Jesus. They were invented by the church long after Jesus had died."

"Not in the Bible? That sounds crazy."

"I know, with all this talk of Heaven and Hell going on it sounds ridiculous, but it's true. I'll be talking about it during my lectures."

"So you're an atheist?"

"Well, I'd say kind of an agnostic-atheist mix."

"What in the world does that mean?"

"For me the words mean two different things. Agnostic has to do with what you can know. I don't really *know*, one way or the other, if there's a God, because, well, it's not the kind of thing you *can* know, like that the sky is blue or fire can burn you. Atheist has to do with what you believe. I don't happen to *believe* in the Christian God. Does that make sense?"

She shook her empty beer bottle and smiled sheepishly. "I don't think my brain is working too good right now."

"You must be exhausted. I'm sure you'd like to get settled in. I could leave."

"No, no, stay. I kind of like talking to you. I haven't talked to anybody, I mean really talked to them, in the longest time." She paused. "Can I ask you another question?"

"Sure."

"Where you came from—your daddy, your kin going way back.... Jesus and all that, it's been their whole life. What happened to you?"

Bart smiled. "I really don't know. What happened to you?"

"You mean about being a lesbian?"

"Yeah."

Jennifer shrugged. "I don't know. It's just the way I am."

"Me too. See what I mean about having things in common?"

"What does your daddy say about you?"

"Lost soul, that kind of thing."

"What if he's right?"

"Then I'm a goner."

Jennifer straightened in her chair. "You say it like it's nothing. Aren't you worried?"

"No. Are you?"

Jennifer lowered her head. "A little. Maybe a lot."

Bart nodded. "I get it. It's not an easy thing to deal with." He crossed his arms and tugged at his right earlobe. "Maybe I can help you out with that."

"How?"

"I wasn't going to mention it in my lectures, but I can squeeze in a few words about homosexuality in the bible. It's quite fascinating, actually. It'll give you something to think about."

"Am I going to want to hear it?"

"You're just going to have to wait and see, now won't you?" He smiled. "I'd better get going. Can I show you the church?"

"Not while I'm drunk."

"Tomorrow then."

Jennifer opened her mouth to speak, then froze.

For a moment Bart waited. He took her hand. "Jenn, did you want to say something?"

Jennifer flashed a forced smile. "It's nothing. It's just … well I know you're not a believer, but I just want to say … I guess I am. Maybe not the way your daddy is, but, well, I don't know, there's got to be more than flesh and bone, you know what I mean? Anyway, I just wanted to tell you, that's all. I hope it doesn't change anything about me being here and all."

"Of course not."

"Good. I'm glad."

"See you tomorrow, around noon? The work crews are all coming around one. Remember, stay inside, at least for now."

"Will do." She pressed her lips together. Her eyes filled with tears. "I don't know what I would have done if you hadn't taken me in."

"I'm glad you're here. We're going to get through this, okay?"

Jennifer forced a smile and nodded.

Bart gave her a hug. "I'll see you tomorrow."

Late the following morning, Bart headed out to his church. He parked next to his new sign and pushed on the frame—rock solid. From his back seat he extracted a bag of stick-on letters and the large rectangular piece of plywood. Having begrudgingly abandoned his "Institute for the Study of Jesus" and still without a replacement name, he stared vacantly at the plywood.

He thought of Jennifer's father, Calvin, whom he had spotted yesterday at the hardware store. His appearance had shocked Bart. Having not seen him for almost ten years, he'd expected to see an older-looking man, but Bart had barely recognized him—gaunt, hunched over, sallow skin, wisps of thin gray hair hanging over his forehead, and lines carved deeply into his face. He couldn't be a day over fifty but had looked an unhealthy seventy-five. The loss of his wife and the ravages of alcohol abuse had clearly taken their toll, but how in the world can a father strike his own daughter? Fortunately, Bart had managed to control his rage and escape notice.

He squeezed his eyes shut—time to focus on the task at hand. Sarah's advice rang in his ears—keep it simple, down-home, relatable. He thought of "The Story of Jesus" but immediately ruled it out for sounding like a children's book. After several other failed attempts, he finally came up with a title he thought he could live with:

Bible Study—Jesus and the New Testament

Bart Trask, Department of Religious Studies

UNC at Chapel Hill

The phrase "Bible Study" made him wince, but it was the best he could come up with. A few minutes later he looked at the sign from the side of the road. The letters could be larger, but all-in-all, it looked pretty good.

He drove to the back of the church and phoned Jennifer. No answer. He knocked at the back door and entered. "Hello?" The bedroom door was slightly ajar. He lightly tapped on it. Nothing. He considered peeking in but decided against it. Surely she couldn't have left. He rushed into the church. "Jenn?"

He found her sitting in the far corner in the back row, to his left. She greeted him with a wave and a sad smile. He sat next to her. The discoloration under her left eye and cheek had become more prominent.

"Did you sleep well?"

"I did, eventually. I had a hard time falling asleep with all the noise running around in my head, but when I did, I slept solid. I just awoke about an hour ago."

"Did you get something to eat?"

She grinned. "Cheerios, right out of the box, and bottled water."

"Was the porta potty okay?"

She grimaced.

Bart laughed. "Don't worry, the work crews will have this place up and running by the end of the day."

"You sure they're not from around here?"

"I'm sure. I checked. Don't worry. They won't know you."

Her face brightened. "Hey, I'm planning on doing some more cleaning this afternoon in the church."

"Thanks, but I'd suggest you wait until after the cleaning service gives the place a once-over on Friday."

"Are you sure there's still going to be stuff to do?"

Bart smiled. "I'm sure. Lots of stuff."

"I know what you told me, but I still feel so bad I can't pay you at least something for all the things you bought."

"I appreciate that, Jenn, but your money is no good here. Besides, like I said, you'll get the chance to pay me back in other ways."

"Yeah, well maybe it would make me feel better."

"Who knows, maybe one day I'll need some help and you'll be there for me. If it never happens, that's okay too because I've got to tell you, without even knowing it, you've already given me a lot."

"What are you talking about? I've hardly done anything."

"Not true. You've given me the chance to help somebody who really needs it. You can't buy that feeling. I'd say that makes me a pretty lucky guy."

Jennifer lowered her head and smiled. "It's funny. Your daddy pretty well said the same thing in church a couple of weeks ago."

"That doesn't surprise me. He's always saying that."

"You're not making fun of him, are you?"

"No, not at all. When he says stuff like that, he actually means it, and lives it. One winter, I think it was a year before I went off to school, he was asked to help out at some homeless shelter in Birmingham. After spending a couple of Saturday afternoons there cooking and serving food, he came home, sold his car, a nice, almost new sedan, donated half the money to the shelter, and bought himself a shit-box replacement."

"Wow, I didn't know that."

"Nobody else does, either. The only reason I do is because of my mother telling me, half frustrated, half proud of what he'd done."

"Your daddy, he's a good man, isn't he?"

Bart nodded emphatically. "Yes, he is."

"I still don't understand why you're not doing it in his church. Did you ask him?"

"No."

"But if it's about Jesus…. You don't say anything bad about him, do you?"

Bart grinned. "No. My father just doesn't think it's right to study Jesus the way professors like me study him."

Jennifer frowned. "There's a certain way?"

"It's all in the lecture. You'll see."

"I bet he's pretty sore you're doing it down the street from him."

"He's not too happy about it."

"Then why—" Jennifer shook her head. "Never mind."

"Why am I doing it here?"

"I guess."

"Like I said, it's a long story."

That evening, even with the warmth of Sarah's body on him, Bart couldn't shake Jennifer's question. These days it was never far from his mind, but coming from her, it felt different. He felt a vaguely sick feeling in the pit of his stomach. He squeezed his eyes tight, rolled over, and begged for sleep.

After a late breakfast with Junia, Bart enjoyed an extended playdate with little Thomas. They wrestled, built castles, raced cars, and played hide-and-seek in and around the house. Two hours later, Bart flopped onto the couch, sweating and grinning from ear to ear. While playing with this little five-year-old bundle of energy, the cares of the world seemed to vanish.

With both Junia and the little guy napping, Bart sat at the kitchen table and stared at a blank Word document. An hour later, after a few false starts, he managed to come up with a sketch of each lecture.

Junia joined him at the table. "He's still sleeping. It looks like you wore him out."

Bart chuckled. "I could barely keep up with him."

She glanced at the screen. "How goes it?"

"It goes."

"I'm sure you're going to be great. You always are in front of an audience, just like Father."

"Thanks." Bart paused. "Ah, listen, I've got something to tell you. Can you promise to keep a secret? I mean really promise?"

"Sure. What is it?"

"A couple of days ago, Sarah and I were fixing the sign in front of the church when somebody came walking down the street...."

Junia listened intently. Her eyes filled with tears. When Bart had finished, she threw her head back and exhaled. "Is there something I can do? Can I see her?"

"I'll have to check with her. I'll let you know."

In the car he called James. "How's Father?"

"Cranky, thanks to you."

"He'll be just fine. He always is. I have a favor to ask. Do you still do the Wednesday evening service?"

"Yes."

"Great. I was wondering, could you mention the lecture series in church? I know how you feel about it, but since Father is participating, I was hoping you could give us a shout-out."

Bart waited. "James?"

"I'll talk to Father about it."

"Thanks. That's all I can ask."

"Hey, do you remember Calvin Adams? He owns the hardware store in town?"

Bart stiffened. "Yeah, sure. Why?"

"He just called me, asking if I'd seen his daughter, Jennifer. Do you remember her?"

Bart hesitated. "Yes, of course. We babysat her."

"He says she disappeared two mornings ago and hasn't contacted him since. He sounded awfully worried."

Bart clenched his jaw. "She probably just went off with friends. She'll show up soon," he said, doing his best to sound nonchalant. "Please don't forget to ask Father about announcing the lecture series."

"You can still back out."

"Talk to you later."

Bart threw his phone onto the passenger front seat and smacked the steering wheel.

He sounded awfully worried....

That afternoon, Bart stopped at the post office, library, several grocery stores, a bicycle store, two motorcycle shops, and several other small shops on and around Main Street. He then headed to the barbershop he had visited for years as a child. How wonderful it would be to see Big Lou, the town barber, just as he had been all those years ago, laughing at his own silly jokes, handing out candy, and talking about his favorite cartoon characters.

As Bart pulled up to the familiar corner in town, his heart sank. The barbershop was gone, replaced with a laundromat. Across the street, where a bakery had been, a large sign for one of the chain haircut/stylist salons caught his eye. Evidently, the insidious creep of modernity had found even Traskville.

With virtually no other commercial establishments to hit, he walked into the hardware store. As the jingle on the top of the door announced his entrance, his guts tightened. Calvin sat behind the checkout counter staring vacantly down an aisle. He was the last guy Bart wanted at his lectures, but figured it might look suspicious if he didn't ask to hang a poster here, especially since the hardware store was one of the bigger stores in town.

Calvin looked at Bart indifferently. "Bart Trask? Long time no see."

"How are you, Calvin?" Bart pushed out the words, as if spoken by someone else.

"Okay." He looked away.

Bart opened his satchel and removed a poster. "Can I ask you to hang this up in your window? It's an advertisement for a lecture series on Jesus."

"A what?"

"Just something I'm doing in town for folks. Can I put it in your window?"

"Since when does your father need to advertise?"

"My father isn't doing it."

Calvin gave the poster a disinterested glance. "Whatever. Go ahead."

"Thanks."

After hurriedly hanging two posters, one on each side of the main entrance, Bart threw himself behind the wheel and slammed the door. He wondered how he'd managed to get through their brief encounter without strangling the bastard. He knew violence was no way to address Calvin's benign ignorance, his lingering grief, his alcohol abuse, and what was probably an impotent rage against the world, but the tug of his primal self was strong.

His last stop would be the home of the local weekly newspaper, the Traskville Chronicle, located at the far corner of what passed for a shopping plaza. He met the owner of the establishment at the front desk. Emmett Wallace, a stocky man in his early sixties with a head of remarkably thick white hair and a mouthful of conspicuously misaligned teeth, and not looking a day older than when Bart had last seen him ten years ago, gave Bart a bright smile and a strong handshake.

"Well, I'll be darned. Bart Trask. Good to see you."

Bart chuckled. "How are things, Mr. Wallace?"

"Just fine. Now that you're all grown up, you can call me Emmett."

"Looks like you're pretty busy today."

"Yep. It's always like this the day before the Chronicle comes out. What brings you back from the hallowed halls of learning? I'm still sorry you got a bit of a rough send-off way back when."

"Thanks, but it's okay; it was a long time ago. I'm just back for a visit, and a little business." Bart retrieved a poster from his satchel. "I'm giving a lecture series in town. Can you find a corner in your rag to advertise it? I've got the particulars here."

Emmett glanced at the notice. "The old Stafford place? That place has been dead for a couple of years."

"Yeah, well, Pastor Stafford is bringing it back to life."

"You doing this with your daddy?"

"Nope."

"Good for you. He must be proud. I'd be happy to give it some space. I'll even come if I can."

"I hope so."

As Bart left the office, he thought about the call James had received from Calvin and grimaced. He drove back to Junia's place, determined to give himself a respite from the heaviness of it all, at least for the evening. Perhaps he could read little Thomas a bedtime story.

13

Late the following evening, at Junia's kitchen table, with his sister and nephew fast asleep, Bart completed his preparation for the lecture series. With the advice of Sarah ringing in his ears, he spent most of his time trying to make the content, which itself was second nature to him, understandable, interesting, and above all, non-threatening to his hometown audience.

He sipped his tea and glanced at the finished product. Was it understandable, interesting, and above all, non-threatening? He hoped so. He had done his very best to bury himself deep into his audience's point of view, but had he succeeded? Was that even possible for anybody? He would find out soon enough.

A light knock at the side door startled him. He jumped up, glanced at Junia's closed bedroom door, crept toward the side door, slightly pulled back the curtain over the small window, and opened it. James stood before him. "Can I come in?" he whispered loudly.

Bart once again glanced at Junia's door, stepped outside onto the wooden porch, and gently closed the door behind him. "What are you doing, scaring me like that? Is everything okay?"

"I just dropped in at the Stafford church on the way home from Bible study, on the off-chance that you might be there, working. I didn't see your car in the back, so I started to leave, but then I heard a kind of thud, or knock, or something like that coming from the living area. I thought somebody may have broken in. I peeked in through the backdoor window but saw nothing other than a dim light in the corner of the room. I figured it was just the old place creaking and groaning, so I started to leave again, but then I heard another faint thump of some kind. I reached for my phone to call you. Then I saw her."

The disclosure knotted Bart's stomach. "Saw who?"

"What the heck is Jennifer Adams doing in there?"

"She didn't see you, did she?"

"No. Why didn't you tell me when I asked you?"

Bart looked toward the house. "Can we sit in your car? I've got a story to tell you."

He told James everything, starting from their chance meeting on the side of the road. When Bart had finished, his brother shook his head. "Who else knows?"

"Sarah and Junia."

"You told Junia?"

Bart touched his brother's shoulder. "Look, I wanted to tell you, but—"

James knocked the hand away. "But what, you thought I'd disapprove of you taking her in?"

"No, but I thought you might tell Father because of what happened to her."

"What are you worried about? You think he'd run off and tell Adams?"

"I don't know. When was the last time he lied, to anyone?"

"This is different. He wouldn't have said a word."

"Yeah, well, let's just say I didn't want to take that chance. Jenn is trusting me to keep her safe until she can move on. I'm trying not to betray that trust. Do you understand that?"

"Of course I understand. It's just.... Never mind, you're right. I'm sorry I got angry."

For several moments, they stared out the front windshield, saying nothing. A dog barked in the distance. Bart again turned to his brother. So, now that you know...."

"I won't say a word to him."

Bart firmly grabbed his brother's forearm and looked straight into his eyes. "You promise, as God is your witness?"

James's eyes widened. "You don't fool around, do you?"

"Whatever it takes. Do I have your promise?"

"Yes, you have my promise."

Bart released his grip. "Thank you."

They sat in the car for several minutes, Bart staring straight ahead with unfocused eyes, James looking out the open side window, saying nothing. The crickets sang out loud in the night sky.

James started his car. "I'd better get back."

Bart began to step out, then turned toward his brother. "I'm sorry I didn't tell you."

"It's okay. I understand."

"You know, for an evangelical, you're alright, almost."

James smiled. "You're lucky I am an evangelical, or else I'd tell you where to go."

"That would be the day."

Bart jumped out and watched his brother drive off.

Bart, Sarah, and Jennifer spent much of Saturday adding some final finishing touches to the sanctuary and Jennifer's secret little condo. A queen mattress, television, and standard-size refrigerator were ordered with Pastor Stafford's approval, scheduled for delivery from Birmingham the following week. To celebrate their progress, they had pizza and beer and played charades. Bart marveled at Jennifer's transformation. With each visit she stood a little taller, her eyes became a little brighter, her smiles—initially mouth-only, tentative, even sad—became full and frequent, and her hugs became tighter and longer.

When the time came Saturday evening for Bart and Sarah to leave, Jennifer threw her hands up to her mouth. Tears streamed down her cheeks onto her slender fingers. "I wish I could show you how much this means to me."

Sarah hugged her. "You're doing it right now."

Bart kissed her on the cheek. "Take care, sweet lady. Don't forget, the stuff is coming on Tuesday. Call me if there are any issues. We'll see you next Saturday for the lecture."

"When are you going back?"

"Tomorrow afternoon, after church."

Church service proceeded uneventfully. If Theodosius noticed Bart and Sarah sitting in their same spot, surrounded by all the same people, he gave no indication of it. Bart was hoping for a shout-out for the lecture series, but none came. Immediately after the service concluded, his father disappeared into the back of the church.

———〰———

The week in Chapel Hill flew by, occupied by all things academic for a young associate professor. On Friday evening, he and Sarah headed back to Traskville. After a restful sleep at Junia's place, an enormous breakfast, and an epic playdate with Thomas on Saturday morning, Bart and Sarah drove to the church. On the way over, Sarah turned to him.

"Are you nervous?"

"Nope."

"Even with your father there, breathing down your neck?"

Bart smiled. "Even with my father there."

Two hours before his lecture, due to start at one o'clock, Bart briefly ran through his notes at the podium. To his surprise, he did begin to feel a little anxious. He recalled a friend in Chapel Hill who, after making it on Broadway, said he felt far more nervous coming back to perform at his hometown high school theatre than at the Richard Rogers Theatre. At home it was personal; he knew the people in the seats. At the time the remark didn't mean much to Bart, but it suddenly hit home.

As he prepared, Jennifer and Sarah buzzed around the locked church like whirlwinds, attending to the food and refreshments, folding programs, placing fans and flowers in the right places, testing the microphone, and setting up the recorded music, a collection of hymns to be played as people filed in.

Sarah handed Bart a program. "Ready to go?"

"I'd say so."

"Jennifer seems pretty excited. It feels good to have her here, doesn't it?"

Bart smiled. "More than I can say."

"It's too bad she won't be able to watch the performance."

"She'll be able to hear it, and even see part of the audience, through a small peep-hole in her bedroom if she can see past my behind."

"You think her father is going to show?"

"I hope not."

Sarah spotted Jennifer approaching them. "Have you told her about James?" she quickly asked in a hushed tone.

"No."

"Are you going to tell her?"

"No, it'll freak her out, maybe even—"

Jennifer joined them. "That should do it. The rest is up to you."

Bart glanced at his watch. "It's noon, Jenn. I'll be opening the doors in a half-hour."

"I know. I'd better go into hiding."

"I'm sorry."

"Don't be. I'll be listening."

After a few last-minute preparations, Bart double-checked both locks on the back door leading out from the living quarters into the yard. He found Jennifer sitting on the bed, poised to take her seat in front of a rectangular hole in the bedroom wall, likely used for a wire or cable, large enough for just a single eyeball, affording a partial view of the podium and audience. An aluminum bucket containing ice and a six-pack of beer sat next to the chair.

Bart grinned. "Looks like you're going to have the best seat in the house."

"How do you feel?"

"Ready to go."

Jennifer looked through the hole. Her eyes suddenly sprang open. She abruptly pulled back.

"What is it? Don't worry; they can't see you."

"He's here."

"Who? Your father?"

She nodded. "Damn him. What's he doing here?"

Bart took a look. The sanctuary was about half full. He spotted Calvin in the second row, to their left. Junia and Sarah sat in the front row, to the right of the podium. No parents, no James. He checked his watch: 12:55. "I'd better get going."

Bart entered the church, went directly to the podium, and scanned the audience. Scattered murmurs greeted him. A steady trickle of people continued to stream in. As he took one final look at his notes his head shot up. His parents and James had just walked in and slid into the back row to Bart's left. The church was now full.

Relax, just be yourself.

He tapped on the microphone. "Good afternoon, folks. Welcome. Thanks for coming to today's lecture, entitled: Jesus—A Historical Perspective. For those of you who may not know me, I'm Bart Trask, son of Linda and Pastor Theodosius Trask. I'm a historian. I teach the history of early Christianity in the Department of Religious Studies at the University of North Carolina at Chapel Hill."

A benign hum filled the air. "As you can see in the program, I'll be discussing the history of Jesus over the next four Saturday afternoons. Each lecture will be divided into two thirty-minute sections separated by a fifteen-minute intermission. Pastor Theo and I will be happy to answer your questions both prior to the intermission and after my final remarks. Pastor Theo will then bring the session to a close with his final comments."

Scattered small pockets of muted chatter and nods of approval suddenly emerged from the audience. Bart glanced at his father. He sat quiet, his head bowed.

"During the question periods, please don't hesitate to speak up. I greatly value whatever you have to say and want to hear it, all of it. I'll also hang around after the lecture for any further unanswered questions. The question periods are very important to me, and not just because your questions deserve to be answered. They're important because they can bring to my attention any concerns from you I may not have considered, and even challenge me to reconsider what I think, so please don't hesitate to ask." He glimpsed Sarah. She gave him a reassuring smile.

"Today, I'll be starting us off with a few words about what a historian of early Christianity, such as myself, actually does, and why we do it. After the break I'll dive into the early life of Jesus, including his birth, home, parents and family, education, and religious beliefs. With the short time we have together over the next four weeks, I'll just be scratching the surface of this huge topic, but I think I can give you at least a feel for it."

Bart surveilled the people before him for a moment. "Jesus—A Historical Perspective. No doubt some, if not most of you, are bewildered by the title, and what I'll be discussing. What in the world do I mean by 'historical perspective'? Why not just say I'm here to talk to you about Jesus? After all, we know that the Bible, written two thousand years ago, is historical, don't we?" He paused. "Well, that depends on what we mean by history. Most folks have a kind of, well, common sense notion about it. Everything that happened in the past is historical, right? If we believe that everything we read in the Bible actually happened, well, then it's history, *all* of it. Actually, that's not quite right."

Bart cleared his throat.

The time has come.

"Events recorded from the past, including those we read in the Bible, can only be considered historical if we can *show* they probably happened, based on *evidence*. It doesn't mean if we have no evidence the event didn't happen. It just means we can't call the event historical. For example, at some point in his life Jesus took his first steps, but even though we *know* it happened, we can't call those first steps a historical event because we have no record of it. You see what I mean? My job today, as a historian, will be to identify events in the life of Jesus that can be considered historical, that is, that can be shown to have probably occurred, based on evidence."

Out of the corner of his eye Bart saw an arm toward the back of the sanctuary momentarily shoot up then rapidly pull back. "Now, this is all fine and good, but as you all know, the Bible doesn't just report what happened, it also makes statements of faith. So what does the historian think about the many faith claims we find throughout the Bible? For instance, take the statement—Jesus was crucified and died for the sins of the world. What can we say about that? Well, since the crucifixion and death of Jesus were events that could have been actually witnessed and recorded, we can decide, based on the evidence, whether we can call these events historical. Most historians, myself included, feel that we can. Therefore, the crucifixion and death—"

The arm shot up again. An elderly woman with long curly white hair stood. Bart recognized her as a substitute teacher from high school. A slightly wavering, breathy voice filled the quiet sanctuary. "If it's in the Bible, it happened. End of story." She resumed her seat to a chorus of "Amen."

Bart gave his teacher a nod. "So the crucifixion and death are historical, but the *belief* that Jesus died for the sins of the world, even if it's true, cannot be called historical, because it's not an event. It's what Christians believe about what the death of Jesus meant, based on faith. It may feel like history to the believer, but it's not. A Christian and a Jew may have different beliefs on whether Jesus is God; that's religion, but they should agree, for the most part, on which events in the life and times of Jesus are historical. I'm not saying religious claims that Jesus performed miracles or is God are not true. For all we know, they are true. They just can't be called historical. You see the difference?"

A collective buzz of whispers and mumbles rolled through the audience. "Now, I know what you're probably thinking. Who cares whether something in the Bible can be called historical? You reason that since the Bible is the divinely inspired Word of God, you already *know* it's true; who needs evidence when we have God's truth? Some of you may even be thinking the only reason historians like me are up to these shenanigans about history is to try to somehow cast doubt on the true Word of God. 'What other reason could there be?' you ask. Well, I think the answer may surprise you. It is true that a small number of New Testament historians may be interested in challenging the faith, but the overwhelming majority are actually devout Christians who study the New Testament in this way, as *historians*, to better inform their own faith, even strengthen it."

A group of three elderly women, affectionately known by all as the "Traskville Crossing Guard Ladies," entered the sanctuary. Bart smiled broadly. "Welcome ladies." He waited until they squeezed in toward the front to Bart's right.

"How can studying the *history* of Jesus better inform the faith? It may sound strange, but it does so by causing us to focus on stuff that we ordinarily don't notice. The thing is, most devout Christians tend to pay a little more attention to the statements of faith and a little less attention to the actual events described in the Bible. That's just fine. It's a great way to read the Bible as a Christian, but when you focus on the statements of faith, important historical information can be easily missed even though they're right there on the page. You can easily discover this for yourself. Just line up the versions of any particular story repeated in multiple gospels and read them side by side. By briefly focusing on the events themselves and not the religious claims, you'll probably discover lots of details that you may not have noticed. For instance, let's briefly consider the birth narratives we find in—"

"Your problem is you don't believe. You gotta see every-thing to believe it."

Bart turned to the voice to his right toward the back of the church. A tall, thin, middle-aged woman with strikingly red hair whom Bart recognized as the high school secretary stood glaring at him with big angry eyes. For a brief moment he considered ignoring the comment and reminding the audi-ence that he couldn't answer questions until the break, but decided this may do more harm than good. He smiled. "Mrs. Cole, it's good to see you. Thank you for coming. What I hap-pen to believe or not believe—"

"You don't have the faith. That's the problem, pure and simple."

Bart held his smile. "That may be, but as a historian I'm just focusing on those events from the past that we can *show* happened based on evidence that most everyone can agree on. If believing an event took place requires faith, that event can't be called historical. I'm not saying the event didn't happen; it's just not history." He scanned the audience. "I appreciate the comment; it's a great one, but if you could, please hang on to any further comments or questions until just before the intermission or the end of the talk."

Bart glanced at his notes. He wondered what his father was thinking. "All right, to show you what I mean about how important details can be easier to see when stories are com-pared side by side, let's briefly compare the birth narratives of Jesus found in Matthew and Luke. In both accounts, Jesus is born in Bethlehem. In Luke, Mary and Joseph travel from their hometown, *Nazareth*, to Joseph's ancestral home of Beth-lehem for a worldwide census decreed by Caesar Augustus.

Shortly after arriving in Bethlehem, Jesus is born. He remains in Bethlehem for only about forty days, returning back to Nazareth after visiting the Temple in Jerusalem.

"In Matthew, there is no report of a worldwide census or travel from Nazareth. Mary gives birth to Jesus in her hometown of *Bethlehem*. Based on information provided by the Maji and others, King Herod determines that Jesus must have been born sometime within the previous two years. In an attempt to kill Jesus, Herod orders the death of all infants up to two years of age in Bethlehem, where Jesus had been living, but the family escapes and flees to Egypt. After Herod's death they intend to return to their hometown of Bethlehem, but reroute to Nazareth to escape the wrath of the King's son.

"As you can see, comparing the stories side by side is a great way to discover details that may have flown under the radar. Now they're jumping off the page. You may also sometimes find, as we have here, some details that don't seem to completely match up, such as the time spent by Jesus outside of Nazareth. I'll have more to say about that later."

"I'm sure you will," called out Bart's substitute teacher, to a chorus of scattered grumbles.

Bart smiled inwardly. He had asked for this, hadn't he? "So how much can we learn about Jesus? Well, the news is good and bad. The good news is that we know quite a bit. For someone who lived two thousand years ago, we have way more historical information on Jesus than anyone else who lived at that time. The bad news is we don't have as much information as we'd like, and the evidence we do have can sometimes be unclear, even downright confusing, as you saw in my example."

Theodosius cleared his throat. The all too familiar distinct, forcible exhalation, sharp and loud even from the back row, cut through the momentary silence of the suddenly tiny sanctuary, turning heads. Bart pretended not to notice.

"You'd think evidence about Jesus would be an easy thing to evaluate. After all, it's just sitting there on the page, almost entirely within the Gospels, for all to see, isn't it? Well, believe me, it's not that easy. Think of how difficult gathering evidence can be in a jury trial. First of all, often times we don't have enough information. Second, what information we do have may or not be reliable. It's amazing how the eyewitness testimony of a car accident, or most other events, can differ between different observers. And finally, if that's not bad enough, we have to consider the effect of personal bias. The truth is, what we happen to believe can sometimes make it harder to see the truth. Just ask a Democrat and a Republican to comment on current events."

Bart stopped for a sip of water. As if on cue, three men from the middle of the audience whom Bart recognized but couldn't place abruptly rose and left. One of the men tossed his program into the aisle, causing a brief uproar. Bart waited, holding a placid expression, until they were gone.

"These problems, and others, exist when doing any kind of history, but they're especially troublesome when studying an ancient text such as the New Testament, written two thousand years ago. Have you ever played the game telephone, when you tell somebody a brief story, and they tell someone else, who tells somebody else, and so on, until you get to the last person who then compares her story with what you told? Isn't it amazing how the stories come out so different, even for a small group of people in the same room, at the same time who have the same education, speak the same language, and share the same culture?"

Bart paused. Among mostly blank stares, he did manage to find a few scattered nods of recognition. This was good. Time to get a little bolder with his audience.

Choose your words carefully. You want them coming back.

"Now compare that with the Gospels we have today. Most historians agree that they were written thirty-five to sixty-five years after Jesus died by people of a different language and culture scattered throughout the Roman empire, copied by hand over and over and over again for hundreds of years by mostly untrained scribes, then translated, oftentimes poorly. It's no wonder that it can be super-challenging to sort out which of the stories we read about are historical, which are not, and why they're not. In our later lectures we're going to dive right into this when we discuss topics such as how Jesus behaved on the cross, the Passover meal, and when Jesus actually died. I'm going to be honest, you may be in for a few surprises. How it affects or informs your faith, if at all, well that's up to you, but if you're willing to play historian with me for the next little while, I think you may find it interesting and worthwhile."

Bart glanced at his father. Theodosius sat straight ahead, stone-faced. If his blood was boiling, he wasn't showing it.

"So how do historians decide what information in scripture should be considered historical? For starters, we do our very best to minimize our personal bias. It's not easy—after all, we are human—but it's important to make the effort. If you could, for the time we spend together, I'd like you to do the same. Try not to focus on what you *believe* but rather on the events themselves. Try to see the events at face value. Believe me, if I were talking to a group of Muslims or Jews or even atheists, I'd be saying the very same thing. In fact, I have said this very same thing to these groups. When you walk out of here, you can snap back into the faith, but for now, I'm hoping you're willing to play along."

A sharp knock, as if something or someone had bumped into a wall, came from behind Bart, where Jennifer was listening. He suddenly thought of her father in the audience and caught his breath.

"Historians have also developed specific guidelines, called historical criteria, that can help us. Don't be scared off by the fancy label. In the jury box, and even in your day-to-day life, you use these same guidelines all the time to figure stuff out. You just don't realize it; it's built into your common sense. I'd like to take a minute to briefly go over a few of these."

Bart wondered, had the noise frightened poor Jenn? He imagined her thinking of her father in the audience and disappearing under the bed like a frightened rabbit.

"The first guideline is about factors that affect the reliability of the evidence. Having direct eyewitness testimony is ideal. The time when the events in question took place is also an important factor. The more recent the events, the better. The length of time between the events and the testimony of the events is also important—the less time the better. It's amazing how quickly things can be forgotten or mixed up. Now all this doesn't mean that evidence given from people who are not eyewitnesses, events from long ago, or testimony given long after the events themselves can't be accurate; it just tends to make it tougher to know.

"The number of independent witnesses, folks who saw the same stuff but didn't talk to each other, is also important. Of course, the more people you have, the better. Think of a car accident. The more direct eyewitnesses who haven't spoken to each other about what they saw, the more likely you'll be able to figure out who hit whom, and who was at fault."

Bart glanced at his family. His mother gave him a reassuring nod. James appeared to be looking at someone to his left. His father glared at him.

"The next guideline is a little tricky. It's when the evidence somebody gives is not what they would *want* to give. That kind of evidence is really strong. So if a tennis player claims her opponent's serve was out of bounds, well, that's one thing, but if she says it wasn't, that's another.

Bart glanced at his notes, but he saw nothing but his father's cold stare.

What is he thinking?

"The last guideline I'll mention is kind of obvious. It's when part of the evidence doesn't seem to fit the life and times of the events. This one tells you right off the bat there's something fishy. For instance, if we find a book claiming to be written by one of the disciples who says he drove his motorcycle to the temple, or a report stating that Thomas Jefferson wrote the Declaration of Independence on his laptop, you'd say wait a minute, that can't be right.

"These, and others, are the tools in the historian's toolbox used to try and figure out what probably happened in the past. I'd like to stop here for questions on what the New Testament historian does and why we do it."

Theodosius rose and joined Bart at the pulpit. Bart tried

to make eye contact with his father, but Theodosius looked straight down the center aisle. Bart scanned the audience. "After your questions, we'll take a fifteen-minute break for refreshments. In part two, we'll dive right into the early life of Jesus."

An elderly woman in the third row slowly stood and raised a crooked arm. Bart lifted his open hand toward her and smiled. "Yes, Mrs. Abercrombie...."

She straightened as best she could and cleared her throat. "Young man, I know you've got all this education and all that, but when it comes to the Bible, the Word of God, you can be sure Pastor Theo has got it covered, *all* of it, history, religion, the whole thing, right from the pulpit." The audience exhibited a collective smattering of heads nodding and statements of "yes indeed" and "Amen."

Bart glanced at his father. Theodosius remained quiet and still. "Thanks so much for that comment, Ma'am. I trust your family is doing well?"

"They're standing here right next to me, for how long, I don't know."

Bart shared a muted chuckle with the audience. "I agree that as a pastor my father has a *vast* knowledge about Jesus as a *religious* figure. Of course my father also knows history, but even he would admit it's not his specialty. To fully understand the *history* of Jesus, we need the historian, whose training and focus is on the history, not the religion. I know that's a hard notion to accept, but if you give me a chance, I think I'll be able to show you what I mean. Remember, you've really got nothing to lose, right?"

Mrs. Abercrombie pursed her lips, shook her head, and sat.

Bart waited for a rebuttal from his father. Nothing came. Bart scanned the group for other questions. A young man in the third row, whom Bart didn't recognize, stood. "Maybe what you say about not paying attention to some historical stuff here and there is true, but since your daddy tells us all we *need* to know about Jesus, who cares about the stuff we may be missing? If it ain't broke...." A cluster of chuckles reverberated through the audience.

Bart nodded. "Sure, if you feel you're getting everything you need to know about Jesus, then why bother looking elsewhere? But if it's possible that a different approach, one you could use *together* with your faith, could increase your knowledge about the life and times of Jesus, why not give it a whirl? What Christian wouldn't want to know as much as possible about the man behind the faith?"

Calvin Adams rose. "I hate to interrupt all this fancy talk about history and all, but there's something bugging me ever since you dropped off that poster for this thing."

Bart stiffened. He forced a smile. "Fire away."

"Maybe it's just me, but I don't think atheists should even be talking about Jesus to a group of God-loving Christians."

The church fell silent. Bart felt a flush of heat rush into his face. With great concealed effort, he threw on a warm, carefree smile, the type of smile he might have chatting with an old friend over a beer. As he locked eyes with Calvin, Jennifer flashed across his mind, unleashing a torrent of silent rage, thumping his temples, tightening his jaw, boiling his bone marrow. He imagined Jennifer recoiling from the peephole. He imagined her feeling the sting of her father's hand on her face. He imagined the terrible helplessness and fear and humiliation she must have felt then, and now, rushing back at her, overcoming her. Bart imagined sprinting off the podium, punching Calvin in the face, and throwing him out on his ass.

"As a historian, whatever I happen to believe or not believe should have no effect whatsoever on what I can show to have likely happened based on the evidence."

"Say it, you're an atheist."

Bart's stomach churned. "I'm not a believer, but as I've just said, that has nothing to do with—"

"So what gives you the right to talk to us about Jesus?"

Bart shrugged. "I don't have any right to talk to you, or anyone else, about Jesus. I've simply invited the good people of Traskville here for a discussion."

"Why do you even want to talk about him?"

Out of the corner of his eye Bart could see his father standing straight as an arrow, motionless, looking out over the crowd. Bart imagined the look on his face, a look he had seen countless times just before his father was about to begin his sermon—head up, eyes bright, lips slightly pressed together, his first carefully chosen word at the ready.

Bart nodded. "It's a good question. Why would a non-believer like me dedicate myself to years of intensive study, reading ancient Greek and other mostly dead languages to learn all I can, so I can teach the history of Jesus and early Christianity? It's really quite simple. Besides being one of the most important people to have ever lived, I find the life and times of Jesus absolutely fascinating." Bart surveilled the audience. "Any other questions on what New Testament historians do and why we do it?"

Calvin's face hardened. He looked around, then abruptly

headed for the door. A family of five, sitting two rows behind him, a middle-aged woman in the row ahead of him, and a number of others, totaling eighteen, left without saying a word. Bart showed no emotion. When the last to leave, a young woman and her two young children, had closed the door behind them, Bart took a quiet deep breath. The damage had been not insignificant, but frankly, could have been much worse. Theodosius continued to look straight ahead, his face relaxed, still as a mannequin.

Bart placed his hand on his father's shoulder. "For those of you who wish to stay, I promise you this—I'll do my best to be informative, and above all, respectful."

An elderly man whom Bart recognized as the town car mechanic during his childhood, sitting in a wheelchair next to the wall to Bart's right, wiggled his crooked wooden cane at him. Bart flashed back to a summer long ago when he briefly worked in Eugene's shop.

"Mr. Setchel. Good to see you."

"I got a simple question for you, young man."

"Please."

"*Why* are you not a Christian?"

Scattered murmurs of approval filtered through the audience. Bart smiled. "It's another good question, but since it's off-topic, I'd be happy to talk to you about it after the lecture if you'd like."

Mr. Setchel gave Bart a dismissive wave. Bart waited for him to leave. He didn't move.

A young man in the middle of the audience stood. Bart recognized him as an employee at Calvin's hardware store. "How you're gettin' anybody to listen to this without falling down dead asleep is what I'd like to know." He smiled and looked around, as if waiting for a laugh. Several people around the man chuckled softly, but to Bart's surprise, most of the audience didn't react. As the man's smile vanished Bart couldn't help but permit himself a grin, fleeting and barely discernable, but noticeable for anyone carefully watching him.

"Don't worry; I have smelling salts."

Laughter filled the sanctuary. Finally, they were laughing with him. He glanced at his father—no response. The young man and two other men of about the same age seated next to him stood in unison and left, the three of them sprinting toward the church door, leaving another small yet conspicuous vacancy. Once again, Bart waited for the church door to creak open and slam shut. No other hands went up. Theodosius remained silent. Bart glanced at his watch. "Let's take a fifteen-minute refreshment break. When we return, we'll discuss the early life of Jesus. Thanks again."

The audience rose and burst into conversation. Bart turned to his father. "I'm surprised you didn't say anything."

"I didn't have to."

"Thanks for not piling on."

"They did my talking for me."

"I suspect we'll both get plenty of questions after I get into the life and times of Jesus. Do you have any prepared comments for the end?"

"I sure do."

"I look forward to hearing them."

Sarah joined them at the podium. "Good afternoon, Pastor Theo."

Theodosius nodded politely. "Good afternoon, Sarah. Excuse me."

They watched him return to his seat. Sarah gave Bart a hug. "Good job. It couldn't be easy talking to Adams."

"I hope my anger didn't show. I'm afraid I was a little curt with him at the end."

"You were just fine." Sarah looked toward the living quarters. "Would you like me to check on Jennifer? I heard a noise."

"Me too. Could you? I'd like to check in with the family."

Junia approached Bart. "Great job. I can't wait for the second half. What did Father say?"

"Nothing."

"Nothing? Wow, that's got to be a first. I guess he's saving it for his final remarks."

"Yeah, well I think I'll go see if I can pull anything out of him."

Bart slid in next to his father. "So tell me, what do you think?"

"I have to say, you are a crafty one."

"What do you mean?"

You'll find out soon enough."

"I hope so." He paused. "Thanks again for being here."

Theodosius rubbed his eyes and ran his hands through his scattered thin strands of graying hair. "I don't object to your use of historical criteria to show what happened in the past. I do object to seeing our Lord Jesus Christ treated in this way, like any other historical figure. Scripture doesn't need your historical criteria to distinguish fact from fiction. God inspired the Bible, therefore, it *is* historically accurate, exactly as it reads on the page. It saddens me to know you don't see that and feel it in your heart."

Bart had heard this, both from his father and from others, many times before. "Are you going to mention that in your closing remarks?"

"Absolutely."

"Good. We can use it as a focus of discussion for the audience."

Theodosius sneered. "You are a glutton for punishment, aren't you?"

"We'll see," Bart said with a grin. He turned to his mother. "You okay, Mom?"

Linda pushed out a smile. "I'm just fine, son."

He headed back to the podium. James caught up with him. "Is Father okay?"

"Just fine. Thanks for coming."

"I've got to know what you're saying to our people."

"I'm not sorry Adams left."

"Yeah, that had to be tough on Jennifer."

"So, what do you think, so far?"

James shrugged. "I agree it's important to know what Jesus did, but it's like Father said, your historical criteria aren't needed here. Jesus is above all that."

Bart nodded. "I hear you. Well, thanks for not throwing tomatoes."

"Hey, if I wanted to do that, I'd be sitting in the front row."

"I'd better go check on Jenn."

He found Jennifer in the kitchen, eating cold pizza. "I heard every word. It was great."

"Thanks. I heard a bump from the bedroom. Everything okay?"

"Sorry, I bumped my knee."

"Do you think I explained myself well enough, I mean for people to understand?"

"Yeah, I think so. I understood you. It was fun to hear all about what historians do, but...."

"But what?"

"It's awfully strange that the story you told about the birth doesn't seem to match up. I mean, it's the Bible. How can that be? Are you sure you're right about all that?"

"I sure am. Check it out yourself. Just pick any story in the Gospels and do a comparison."

"I'm thinking it probably threw them for a bit of a loop. They're probably thinking you're trying to pull some kind of trick or something."

"I hope not."

"How's your father doing?"

"He's disagreeing with me, as usual." Bart glanced at his watch. "I'd better get back. I'll see you later."

As Bart stood at the podium waiting for people to take their seats, his heart sank. More than a few additional people had left at the break. After starting with a full house, it appeared he had now lost about a third of the audience.

He tapped the microphone. "Welcome back. I'd now like to dive right into what we can say about the early life of Jesus from a historical perspective. Before we begin, I'd like to briefly review with you the upcoming lectures, which I hope you can all attend.

"Next Saturday I thought I'd review what Jesus had to say about a few important issues that arose during his ministry. For instance, what makes a person right with God? Jesus's later follower Paul believed having faith in the death and resurrection of Jesus brought people salvation. James, on the other hand, believed that in addition to faith, living a good life and good works are also required. Where did Jesus stand? He had a lot to say about it, and it may surprise you.

"I'll also be touching on what Jesus had to say about the afterlife. Most of us assume he believed in our modern-day notions of Heaven and Hell, but did he? Finally, and this one may sound crazy, but during his ministry, what did Jesus consider to be his relationship with God?"

Hushed murmurs rippled through the audience. "In two weeks, I'll be giving examples from the Gospels showing some of the challenges and limitations the New Testament historian faces. I thought I'd revisit the birth narrative and discuss the Passion to show you how difficult it can be to determine what we can call historical."

Bart glanced at the program. "For my last session, in three weeks, I'd like to talk about what Jesus had to say about a few modern-day issues that affect us. What did Jesus and the writers of the bible say about slavery, the treatment of women, and finally, homosexuality? Traditionally, Christians have believed that the Bible condemns homosexuality, but does it? Once again, I think you'll be surprised to hear—"

"No!"

The entire audience turned toward the back of the church. A man, holding his Bible, sprinted toward the front door, threw it open, and raced out. A moment later, the man's wife and son quickly followed out the door, as if chasing after him. The audience sprang into an uproar.

Bart stood at the podium, frozen, rigid as a post, his face

suddenly soaked in sweat. He opened his mouth, but no words came. People began to leave, initially just a few, but then more, and still more, until in one final frenzied push, they all squeezed out the church door, knocking over the refreshment table on the way out.

Pastor Theodosius Trask, father of Bart Trask, had fled, followed by the entire audience, leaving only Bart, Junia, and Sarah, standing with open mouths in the empty church.

Bart stood frozen at the podium, staring with wide unfocused eyes out through the open church door. Sarah dashed toward him. "Bart, what the hell just happened?"

The door to the living quarters flew open. With disbelieving eyes Jennifer glanced into the empty church, raced to the front door, slammed it shut, locked it, and returned to Bart. "Why did everybody leave like that?"

Junia joined Sarah and Bart. "What got into Father? Why did everyone leave?"

Bart shuffled to the front of the church on legs he couldn't feel. He examined with unseeing eyes the upended table and mess of food and beverages on the floor. Sarah escorted him to the last row of pews. For several minutes, they sat, saying nothing. She placed her hand over Bart's hand and squeezed. He made a feeble attempt to withdraw, but she hung on.

"Bart, listen to me. He did not walk out on *you*. He walked out on your message. Do you hear me?"

"But he insisted on being here … speaking after the lecture … staying for questions. What happened?"

"I don't know. It was when—"

"He took everyone with him. They followed him out, like sheep." He turned his head toward her. "Why did he leave?"

Sarah shrugged. "It's when you were talking about the upcoming lectures. I guess it was just all too much for him."

Jennifer slid in next to Bart. "I'm awfully sorry. Why did he leave?"

Bart shook his head. "I just don't understand it. What happened?"

Junia squeezed his brother's hand. "I have no idea. Something blew his head off. He sprang up as if he'd been bitten by a rattler."

Bart stood. "I've got to get out of here." He sprinted to the door. Sarah followed him. "Where are you going?"

"I don't know. I just need to get away."

As he turned toward the parking lot, he caught sight of his sign. He momentarily froze, then ran toward it. One of the two wooden posts had been severely cracked. The base had been nearly ripped out of the ground. The plywood had been smashed, and most of the letters were gone, scattered on the ground at his feet. He stared at the mess, his body rigid, his mouth open, motionless, oblivious to the cars and trucks whizzing past him. Sarah caught up with him. "Oh no. Bart, I'm so sorry."

Bart lightly touched the fractured post. It collapsed, sending the sign crashing to the hard earth, raising a plume of dust. He slumped to the ground. Sarah flopped down next to him. He picked up a small splinter of wood, weakly poked the hard ground, tossed the splinter away, and turned to her.

"I just can't believe he left."

A breeze came up, blowing several letters toward him. He tossed them back into the breeze. Sarah wrapped an arm around him, saying nothing. For several minutes he looked at the wreckage with vacant eyes. An oil truck raced past them, sending up a whirlwind of dust.

Bart looked at the church. He suddenly stiffened. A moment later, he sprang to his feet. "If he thinks this is going to stop me...."

Sarah jumped up. "Bart, I don't think your father meant to—"

"I've got a lecture to give and I'm going to give it."

She gently grasped his hands. "Sweetheart, please listen to me. Before you do anything, I think you should talk to him. Find out what happened in there. Find out why he left."

He pulled away and began picking up the letters. "Let's clean up this junk and get the tools and materials from the shed. It's a good thing I bought some extra wood. Do you think we have enough cement?"

Sarah grabbed his forearm. "Honey, can we just sit down for a minute and talk this out?"

Bart searched the ground around him. "I can't find the 'Y.' Do you see it?"

Two hours later, they completed their work. The new sign, supported by rope and stakes while the cement hardened, stood tall and straight. The damaged remnants of the old sign and the old cement bases were out of sight, leaving no trace. A warm sun hung in the cloudless late-afternoon Alabama sky. Bart wiped his sweaty face on the sleeve of his white dress shirt, took a few steps back toward the road, looked at their new creation, and exhaled forcefully.

Sarah approached him. "Okay, so now you have your new sign. What now?"

Bart forced a brief smile. "Repeat the lecture next week."

"To an empty church?"

"I'll figure something out. I'll get somebody in there."

"Before you do anything, can you *please* talk to your father?"

Bart turned away from her toward the sign and stared at it. Sarah gently touched him on his cheek. "Sweetheart, I know you're hurting, but I think it's best that you—"

"Can I ask you to put away the tools? I need to speak to Jennifer."

After a restless night, Bart awoke feeling exhausted. Within seconds of gaining consciousness the events of the previous day came rushing back, scorching his insides. As the jumble of incoherency in his racing mind began to clear, a thought emerged. Sarah was right. Before doing anything else, he had to see his father. He had to get to the bottom of this nightmare.

He thought about the lecture series. As much as he didn't want to give his father the satisfaction of blowing it up, Sarah did have a good point. Who could he find to fill the pews? As he mulled over this, a question suddenly sprang up, constricting his insides. With his anger still boiling inside him, he tried to squash it, but the question only became louder.

Is spite ever a good reason to do anything?

Bart covered his face in his hands. Perhaps he should just swallow hard, have it out with his father, cut his losses, and move on down the—

He froze. How could he possibly even think of packing up and going somewhere else? The idea, having lived for a brief second, suddenly felt absurd. The lecture series will proceed in Traskville. It *must* proceed.

Sarah stroked his arm. "Are you okay? You're all sweaty."

"I didn't sleep well."

"Why don't you stay in bed a little longer? I'll try to keep the house quiet."

"I'm going to go see him."

"Good. What are you going to say?"

Bart hesitated. "I don't know."

"How do you feel?"

"Angry."

Sarah wrapped her arm around Bart's waist and pulled herself toward him. "Would you like to talk to me first, you know, just to flesh out your thoughts and cool off a little? It's never good to respond when angry. I could role-play your father."

Bart gently removed her arm and sat on the side of the bed. "Thanks, but no. I'll pull it together when I see him. Besides, you couldn't possibly play him."

"Really? I think I understand him. I don't agree with him about a few things, but I understand him, maybe even better than you."

"I doubt that."

Sarah hopped out of bed and faced him. "Bart, he's not rejecting you as his son, he's rejecting your message. You know damned well the historical Jesus challenges his faith as a fundamentalist. He knows it too, he knows you know it, and he thinks that's why you're giving the lectures. He's angry, and yes, embarrassed in front of his people. He thought he could handle it, but it looks like he couldn't. Please try to understand that."

"I'm going over at one. I'll let you know how it goes."

"Did you hear me?"

Bart headed for the shower.

—⚬⚬⚬—

Bart paused at the front door of the Trask home, took a deep breath, knocked, and entered. He found his mother sitting in her favorite chair next to a large window looking out over her garden. She turned toward him, forced a brief smile, and lowered her head. Bart knelt before her and grasped her hand. "How are you, Mom?"

Tears welled up in her eyes. "I'm sorry," she said softly. "I didn't want to leave."

"It's okay. I understand. It would have been tough for you to stay. Has he said anything?"

"No, but he's so upset. He gave the church service to James this morning, at the last minute. He's never done that."

"He didn't say why he ran out?"

"Not a word. All of a sudden he just stiffened up, almost like a convulsion. That's when he shouted out and left. Your brother and me, we didn't know what to do."

"Is he in? I need to talk to him."

"He's upstairs, talking to James." She took his hand. "Please don't be hard on him."

"Mom, look at me." She slowly lifted her head until their eyes met. "Are *you* upset with me?"

She wiped her eyes and shook her head. "No," she whispered. She looked away. "I'm sorry I left."

"Don't be. It's okay," he said softly. He kissed her on the forehead and headed up the stairs to his bedroom. He hesitated at the door, remembered what Sarah had said, and knocked.

The door flew open. James stood before him with wide eyes. Bart took a single step inside. His father sat at James's desk. For a moment they locked eyes. Theodosius turned his head away.

Bart slowly walked toward the window, looked outside for a few moments, then turned toward his father. "Why did you leave?"

Theodosius averted his eyes. "I couldn't bear to stay, not one second longer."

"You didn't like what you were hearing, so you got up and left. Is that it?"

Theodosius exhaled forcefully. "Jesus is *not* just another historical figure. The Bible is *not* just another historical text. I've told you countless times. Subjecting them to your 'historical criteria,' as if Jesus were not God, and the Bible were not the written Word of God, became more than I could bear."

Bart frowned. "I don't get it. You knew what you were getting yourself into. You'd said it yourself. We've both known, for years, where we stand on this stuff. This didn't *become* more than you could bear. It's been more than you could bear for years, but you never ran out on me before. What happened this time? What was so terrible this time that you had to run for your life?"

Theodosius turned toward the desk, away from his son. "Our private discussions, they were one thing, but to misrepresent the Word of God before our beloved community, it was all just too much."

"I see. So it was all about the audience. You just couldn't bear to watch them listening to a different point of view."

"*That* point of view, coming from my own flesh and blood? No, I couldn't."

Bart felt a rush of heat rise up within him. "So you left, and took everybody with you."

Theodosius turned toward Bart. "What? What do you mean I—"

"Of course you did. You *know* the power you hold over those good people. You had to know that racing out the way you did, as if your pants were on fire, would send them a powerful signal. So off you went, flying out the door, pulling everybody out with you, leaving me standing there, looking like a fool." Bart glared at his father with cold eyes. "Who knows, maybe that's why you came in the first place."

Theodosius jumped up. His face reddened. "I did no such thing. How dare you accuse me of such a thing. Who do you think these people are, puppets under my control? I'll have you know they can think for themselves. I told you why I left. It had nothing to do with anybody else in that sanctuary." He walked toward Bart, stopping only to avoid bumping into him. He pointed an accusatory finger at his son's nose. "If you ever accuse me of deceit again, you will no longer be my son." He brushed past James and flew down the stairs.

James gently closed the bedroom door. He threw his hands up to his head. "Have you lost your mind? You actually accused him of setting you up, a premeditated ambush. How could you do that?"

Bart turned toward the window. His shoulders slumped. He shook his head. "I don't know. It just came out of me. I don't believe it for a second. I'm so sorry."

"Just because you don't like why he left doesn't give you the right to create your own reasons, especially something like that. You owe him a huge apology."

"I know."

"Now!"

"I will. I just wish I understood why he left."

"He told you why he left."

"I heard him, loud and clear, but it just doesn't make any sense. Think about it. If anything, his anger, or embarrassment, or whatever else was running through him should have made him want to stay even more to make sure he had his say while the blasphemy was still ringing in his ears. Believe me, we may be different in some ways, but I *know* him. I know how he thinks. I don't get it."

"He was angry. You're his son. He felt betrayed and embarrassed in front of the community. He figured he could handle it, but he couldn't. Have you ever been so mad you can't see straight? What happens? Everything shuts down around you, doesn't it? There's no calculation; it's all impulse."

Bart peered at his brother for a moment, then headed for the door. "I'll go find him and apologize."

"I'm sorry it all had to end that way, but believe me, it's for the best."

Bart stepped back from the door, closed it, and turned to his brother. "Actually, I plan to continue the lectures," he said softly, almost under his breath.

"What? Where?"

"The same place."

"To an empty sanctuary?"

"We'll see. I'll figure something out."

James threw his arms up. "Oh come on, Bart, you can't be serious. Why? Wasn't yesterday enough? Why don't you just apologize to Father and move on?"

"I don't plan on reaching out to anyone in Traskville. I think I might try to find an outside audience."

"But it's still *in* Traskville, right down the street. Don't you get that?"

"I do get it."

"Then why do it here? The only reason you brought it to Traskville was to give your lectures to the local townsfolk, the people you know. Now that that's gone, why stay, especially after what happened? It's only going to get him angrier with you. Is that what you want, to turn this into some kind of slug-fest? I know you'd love nothing better than to defy him, but, come on, enough is enough."

"James, it's not about defiance, or anything like that."

"Then why stay?"

Bart found his brother's eyes. "Jennifer."

"Jennifer?"

"I can't leave her now. She's been abandoned once already. Her mother is dead. Her father just beat her up. She's got no money. She's afraid to reach out to what little family she has. She's frightened and helpless. She needs a friend and a safe place for the next little while. I promised to watch over her, care for her, keep her safe, until she can leave. I'm not about to walk away from that at a time like this."

"Junia could watch her and provide whatever she needs."

"Are you kidding? Jenn would be gone in a flash if she knew I didn't need her to look after the place. It was the only reason she agreed to stay. She'd be gone in a heartbeat with nothing but the clothes on her back."

"Why don't you bring her up to Chapel Hill with you guys?"

Bart chuckled. "And put her where? We barely have room for the two of us."

"Okay, then find her a small apartment. I'm sure we could help her out."

"She'd never accept that kind of help, not in a million years."

James flopped on his bed. "What does she do in the church, anyway?"

"She keeps the sanctuary clean, prepares the refreshments for the lecture, has a few repair projects going, that sort of thing. You should see her eyes light up when I thank her for the work she's done around the place when I'm gone. I don't think she's ever felt truly appreciated in her life. I don't want to take that away from her, or even mess with it, at least not now."

"Maybe if you tell Father, he'll understand, even help her, so you don't have to."

"And risk blowing her cover? No way."

"What makes you think you're going to get anybody outside of Traskville to show up?"

Bart shrugged. "I'll do my best. At least I can count on Sarah and Junia. Maybe I can even bribe little Thomas to come along. No matter what, I just can't leave Jenn until she's ready to go."

James shook his head. "You know, I don't know whether to love you for trying to help Jennifer or hate you for hurting Father."

"I thought as a Christian you're not supposed to hate anybody."

"Hey, we all have our limits."

"I suppose we do."

"Please go apologize to Father."

"I will."

Bart left their bedroom, his head low with the stinging regret of what he'd said to his father still ringing in his ears. He found his mother in the same place he'd left her, looking out the window, lips pressed together, eyes glistening wet. He kissed her on the cheek. She began to cry.

"It's okay, Mom, it'll be alright."

"He stomped out of here angrier than I've ever seen him. He went off somewhere, I don't know where. He's not answering his phone."

Bart glanced at his watch and grimaced. He had a flight to catch early that evening. "I'll talk to him as soon as I can, I promise."

Bart sat slumped in his car, his head bowed, his insides tied up in knots, staring with wide, unfocused eyes at his hands in his lap. Despite years of discussion, debate, even heated argument with his father, never once had either of them made it personal. Never once had either of them spoken in anger, until now. Bart's accusation, hurled with shameful vitriol, rang in his ears, eviscerating his insides. Suddenly, why his father had fled didn't seem to matter.

He started his car. He stared out the windshield, unable to move, as if the air around him locked him in place. He glanced into the rearview mirror, turned off the car, and squeezed his grieving eyes shut.

Bart and Sarah landed in Raleigh just before eleven that evening. On the drive home from the airport he filled the car with sound—a podcast, music, a comedy channel—anything to distract him from the unshakeable, dissonant cacophony of depressing thoughts, but it didn't much help. On the trip home he'd barely spoken a word. He left his suitcase at the door, went directly into the bedroom, and flopped onto the bed.

Sarah nudged him. "You're not sleeping in your jeans, are you?"

He sat up, shoulders hunched, head drooping. "What a disaster."

"Come on," she said, unbuttoning his shirt. "Let's get you into bed. You're exhausted."

"I just wish I hadn't said those things to him."

She caressed his cheek. "It just got away from you. It happens to all of us."

"Even you?"

"I've had my moments. You'll feel better when you apologize."

Bart peeled off his jeans and crawled under the sheets. "I just don't understand why he left. I feel absolutely gutted for what I said to him, but at the same time, this anger I feel … I just can't seem to shake it."

Sarah sat on the side of the bed. "Listen, I understand why you're angry, but please try to understand how he feels. I know you're trying to open his mind to a different point of view, but pounding on a nail that's already firmly in place doesn't move the nail. Like I said before, this history lesson you're throwing down … it's blasphemy, it's high treason. You may not be making any theological claims directly, but as they say, you don't have to be a weatherman to know which way the wind is blowing. Face it, you're making a case against Christian fundamentalism. Believe me, he gets that message loud and clear, and he doesn't like it."

Bart propped himself up on his elbows. "Maybe, but I shouldn't be blamed for what he makes of it theologically. I'm not in the theology business. I'm just trying to teach a little history about one of the most important people who ever lived. I happen to believe that history matters and that it's good to be as informed as possible about the things we choose to believe."

"Let me ask you something. If the historical Jesus happened to mesh perfectly with the religious claims made about him by your father, would you still feel compelled to do all this? I don't mean keeping the lectures at the church—at this point that's for Jenn—but if it all fit together, would you still be doing it?"

Bart shrugged. "Probably not, because it wouldn't be necessary. If everything matched up, the history would likely be a well-known, accepted part of the theological narrative instead of what it is now, largely dismissed."

"Maybe, but you know what I'm trying to say. Bart, you're not just talking to move the air around. You've got an ax to grind with Christian fundamentalism. You're aiming a razor-sharp dart at a great big target, which we all know includes your father. He knows it too, and he doesn't like it. For him it's not just about what you believe. It's personal. Surely you must see that."

Bart looked away. "Of course I see it," he said quietly.

"Okay, so now we're getting somewhere."

"I take it you don't approve?"

"I didn't say that. I just want you to be crystal clear about what's driving the bus here, so you can make the best possible decisions. When are you going to apologize to him?"

"Soon, I hope. I wish he hadn't run off after we talked."

"I don't see how you're going to get anybody to come to the church."

"We'll see. I don't plan on talking to an empty sanctuary."

She kissed him on the cheek. "Get some sleep, sweetheart. You've had a hell of a day."

For the following week, while preparing for his fall semester, Bart contacted media outlets from multiple cities in both Jefferson and Shelby counties to advertise his newly revised lecture series, a meticulous distillation of the original four lectures into a single two-hour lecture with intermission, given on each of the next three weekends. Presenting a four-part series of lectures on successive weeks may have worked for a local audience, but not for people having to travel longer distances.

However, this created a new challenge. Could he condense the material to fit the time constraint, give the topics a sufficient airing to be informative, and remain casual, interesting, and entertaining? Initially, he had his doubts, but with a nip here and a tuck there, he felt he could, if all questions could be held until after the presentation. After a few false starts, he came up with a new title—The Historical Jesus: How and what history can tell us about an itinerant preacher from Galilee—and completed the revision.

After reaching out to a number of cities, Bart contacted a professor under whom he studied, now at the University of Alabama in the department of Religious Studies, with a request to get the word out to his colleagues and graduate students. Tuscaloosa and Birmingham were both about twenty-five miles from Traskville, a bit of a hike to come for a talk on the historical Jesus, but Bart hoped that his connection with the professor would serve as a sufficient hook to attract the curious and interested. In view of the limited seating and considerable distance some people may be traveling, Sarah set up and managed the allocation of free tickets for the event, scheduled for the next three Saturdays. To his amazement and delight, within twenty-four hours he "sold out" the first two weekends and nearly the third.

Through it all, ruminations of the disastrous lecture and contentious discussion he'd had with his father lingered with such a heaviness, strapped to his back like an invisible bag of cement. The apology he owed his father barely left his mind. Should he call him, or should he wait until the weekend, when they could speak in person? After picking up his phone several times, he decided to wait.

Late Friday afternoon, the day before the lecture, Bart and Sarah returned to Junia's place. They had dinner and a delightful extended playdate with little Thomas. After Thomas had been tucked away in bed, Bart visited Jennifer. She greeted him with a hug.

"It's about time you came back to see me."

He smiled. "Jenn, you're never far from my mind. I trust all is going well?"

"Sure, except for going a little stir-crazy, but I did get a lot done." She grabbed his hand and pulled him into the sanctuary. "Come see." She pointed to the center aisle and down a row of pews. "I gave the floor, all of it, a good scrubbing. You should have seen the color of the water, bucket after bucket.

It looked like mud. I cleaned it before, but nothing like this. How do you like it?"

Bart bent down and took a close look. "What a difference. I thought it was clean before, but now it shines."

"And the pews, I gave them a good going-over too."

Bart ran his fingers over the top of the backrest in the front row. The amber-toned, straight-grained white oak shone as if new. "Wow, the woodgrain is beautiful. These pews probably haven't looked this good in years. How did you do it?"

"With a mountain of cleaning supplies, some products for wood I found in the basement, and a lot of elbow grease. You really like it, and the floor too?"

"I love it! Thanks so much for doing this, Jenn. I couldn't do it without you."

"I'm glad to help any way I can. I told you that."

"Have you heard from Tracy?"

Jennifer smiled. "Yes, a couple of days ago. I told her all about your speech, and what happened. She wants to give you a hug and strangle my father."

"Tell her I'll take the hug." Bart checked the cupboard and fridge. "Looks like you're running a bit low. I'll get you stocked up tomorrow morning."

"I feel so bad. I wish I could pay you back."

"We already had that discussion, remember? If anything, I should be paying you for all the work you've done and for keeping the place together."

"Not a chance." Jennifer leaned casually against the fridge. "Are you nervous about tomorrow?"

"No. I'm actually looking forward to it."

"Did you see your father? I mean, since he stormed out?"

Bart turned his head slightly away. "Right after the lecture."

"How did it go?"

"Not great. I plan to see him after I leave here."

Jennifer lowered her head. "I'm sorry to hear that," she said softly. "Did he say why he left?"

Bart hesitated. "He just didn't agree with what I had to say."

"That's too bad."

Bart brightened. "We'll see you tomorrow, okay?" He gave her a hug.

"What time is the lecture at?"

"Two."

Jennifer kissed him on the cheek. "We'll see you then."

Bart sat in his car, gripping the wheel. The time had come. He called his mother.

"How are you, Mom? I'm back in town."

"I'm worried about your father."

Her abruptness stiffened him. "What's going on?"

"The whole week he's been dragging himself around the house like a zombie."

"Has he said anything to you about, you know, the lecture, or me?"

She exhaled harshly. "Said anything? He barely looked at me yesterday before rushing off to his ... confounded conference in Atlanta with James."

"Don't worry; he's going to be okay. I promise. When are they getting back?"

"Tomorrow afternoon." She began to whimper. "There's something *wrong* with him. I know it. I can feel it."

"I wish I'd realized just how much doing this in public, in front of all his—"

"It's *more* than that, I tell you! I can feel it. Something terrible is happening inside him."

"What do you mean inside him?"

"It's as if something is suddenly eating him alive. Bart, he's dying inside. I can feel it."

Bart caught his breath. He opened the front window. A gust of cold spring air hit his face. "He's not dying, from the inside or any other way. Do you hear me?"

"I *know* him. Do you hear *me*?"

"I do, but—"

"Talk to him. Maybe you can get to the bottom of this."

"I will, I promise, as soon as he gets back. I'll see you both soon."

Bart dropped the phone in his lap.

It's as if something is suddenly eating him alive.

He rubbed his eyes, took a deep breath, and drove off.

The following afternoon, Bart arrived at the church ninety minutes before the lecture. Jennifer had her chair and ice bucket of beer ready. Fifteen minutes before the lecture, the music started. Bart peeked through the hole. The place was already nearly full. To his relief, he recognized no one. Whatever backstage jitters he may have had vanished.

At two o'clock he entered the sanctuary. The collective hushed chatter of the audience ceased. He tapped the microphone. "Good afternoon, folks. Welcome. Thanks for coming. I'm Bart Trask...."

The lecture began smoothly, but it soon became clear that Bart was speaking to two distinctly different groups—one that received him well, and the other that seemed to exude a rather strange mix of bewilderment and disgust. Despite a few defections he was pleased with the first half. The second half of the lecture, as information-dense as it was, sailed along surprisingly well, but was also punctuated with episodic snarls of contempt and the defection of several more people.

"I'd now like to turn our attention to a particular detail regarding the death of Jesus. I think it's another excellent example of how the Gospel writers sometimes took liberties with the historical record in order to express what, for them, was a theological 'truth.'"

A dissonant chorus of murmurs filled the church. Bart glanced at his notes. "According to the Gospels, Jesus is crucified and died during the Passover festival. The question is—when? To answer this question, I'd like us to compare the accounts of this event in the Gospels of Mark and John.

"Before jumping in, I'd like to give you a little background so you can better understand what the Gospels are actually saying. The daylight hours prior to the evening Passover meal is known as the Day of Preparation for Passover. This consists of, among other things, meal preparation centered around the sacrificing of a lamb. The Day of Preparation ends at sundown when the Sabbath begins and the Passover meal is served."

Bart scanned the audience. Apart from a few pockets of hushed chatter, most people seemed to have their eyes locked on him.

"In Mark 14:12 we're informed that on the Day of Preparation, 'when the Passover lamb is sacrificed,' Jesus's disciples asked him where he wanted them to make the preparations for the Passover meal. That evening the disciples eat the Passover meal with Jesus, known to most people as the Last Supper. After supper, Jesus prays in the Garden of Gethsemane, is betrayed by Judas Iscariot, is arrested, appears before the Jewish authorities, and spends the night in prison. The following morning Jesus appears before the Roman governor Pontius Pilate, who, after a few words with Jesus, orders his immediate execution. According to Mark 15:25, Jesus is executed at nine o'clock in the morning, the morning *after* the Passover meal was eaten."

Bart once again scanned the audience. "Is everyone with me?" He saw a smattering of nods. "Excellent. So far, so good. Now let's examine the account of these events in the Gospel of John, the last of our four Gospels to be written. In John, as in the other Gospels, after his meal with the disciples Jesus goes out to pray, is betrayed, arrested, imprisoned, and the next morning is condemned to be immediately executed by Pontius Pilate. It all sounds the same, right? It is, except for two things. John reports that this last meal Jesus had with his disciples took place *before* the festival of the Passover, according to John 13:1. Before the festival? How can that be? John 19:14 also tells us exactly when Jesus was condemned for immediate execution—'Now it was the Day of Preparation for the Passover; and it was about noon.'"

Bart frowned. "The Day of Preparation? What's going on here? According to John—"

"I'm sorry, but I've had just about enough of you trying to convince us that these holy men were liars." An elderly gentleman with a thin, clean-shaven weathered face, slicked-back white hair, and a white dress shirt stood in the third row to

Bart's left. In his right hand he held a brass knob walking stick, and in his left hand he clutched a tweed herringbone flat cap.

"Sir, I'm not calling anyone a liar. I'm simply—"

"I know what you're up to." The man stared at Bart with cold eyes. He spoke slowly, carefully enunciating his words. "It's not going to work."

Although Bart didn't welcome the interruption, wasn't this exactly the kind of challenge he'd wished to receive? With the audience beginning to murmur, he so desperately wanted to engage the gentleman but somehow managed to resist what would have certainly been a lengthy interruption to his prepared remarks. He offered the man a nod of understanding. "Sir, I appreciate your concerns. I'm sure you're not alone. I'm afraid I can't address them now, during the lecture, but I'd love to return to them during the Q & A, and even after the lecture, if you'd like."

"Why not here and now, while this latest accusation is still ringing in our ears?" the man asked, his clear, strong voice echoing in the sanctuary.

Bart stiffened. "I'm so sorry, I really do want to discuss this with you, but in the interest of everyone's time, we *must* move on."

The man shook his head. "I feel sorry for you," he muttered. He slid past the three people next to him and headed for the door with a slow but steady gait, his back straight, his head held high. The audience grew silent as the regular dull thud of cane on wooden floor echoed throughout the sanctuary until finally he reached the front door, emphatically pushed it open, and slammed it behind him.

Bart's heart sank. Such a glorious opportunity wasted. He waited for the scattered murmurs to subside then glanced at his notes. "Alright, so here's the problem. According to John, Jesus was executed at about noon on the Day of Preparation, well *before* the Passover meal later that evening. How can this account be reconciled with Mark's Gospel, which claims that Jesus wasn't even arrested until *after* the Passover meal and was crucified at nine o'clock the following morning? When did Jesus actually die? Did The Last Supper, as we know it, even take place?"

A buzz arose from the crowd. Bart went on. "Although people have tried, the difference can't be easily reconciled, but it can be explained by how John views Jesus. John is the only Gospel that explicitly identifies Jesus as the 'Lamb of God.' In John 1:29, we are told that John the Baptist sees Jesus and declares him to be the Lamb of God who takes away the sins of the world.

"The connection now becomes obvious. It seems likely that John has altered the historical record in order to score a theological point. By having Jesus die in Jerusalem at the hands of the Jewish leaders on the Day of Preparation just like the sacrificial lambs, John is expressing what for him is a theological truth, that Jesus was the ultimate sacrificial lamb of God."

After discussing several other issues Bart brought his prepared remarks to a close on time to an awkward mix of polite and vigorous applause.

"Thanks so much for your kind attention. I'd be happy to take any questions."

A young man stood and raised his hand. At that moment, Bart caught sight of James standing in the back of the church.

"I don't understand why just because Mark, Matthew, and Luke don't record Jesus calling himself God like John does, that he didn't think he was God."

Bart nodded. "It's hard to get into anyone's head, but it seems to me that if Jesus had been making such claims as 'I and my father are one; Before Abraham was, I am; I am the way, the truth, and the life,' claims we find in John, that the writers of the earlier Gospels would have also been aware of these claims and recorded them. The idea that Mark, Matthew, and Luke would not have considered these stupendously important claims from Jesus important enough to mention is inconceivable. Clearly, they would have been the *most* important things to say. I think the best explanation is that John puts these statements on the lips of Jesus, statements the man himself likely never made, to make a strong theological point shared by many in the Christian community at the time John was written, that Jesus was equal to God."

"Yeah, but he sure sounds like God in all the Gospels, I mean with all the miracles and so on."

"Oh, sure. Mark, Matthew, and Luke thought he was divine, the son of God, actually, but there's no historical evidence that Jesus *himself* thought he was God."

Bart entertained several additional questions from a dwindling but enthusiastic audience, the dissenters having all left, before bringing the Q and A session to a close. A small group of people hung around for several further questions. The moment they left, Junia and Sarah rushed to him, applauding.

Sarah kissed him. "Well done! I'm amazed you managed to pack in so much information in such a short period of time without making it feel rushed or like we were in school."

Junia patted him on the back. "That's because he knows this stuff like the back of his hand, *and* he's a brilliant speaker."

Bart forced a smile. "Thanks. I've got to say, I'm rather pleased with myself."

James slowly walked toward them, keeping his hands in his pockets. "I need to speak to you," he said without emotion.

Junia kissed Bart. "Sarah and I are going to rescue Mom from Thomas. He's been a little cranky today. I wonder if he's coming down with something."

Bart glanced toward the living quarters and back to James. "I'll be back in a second."

Jennifer greeted Bart with a long tight hug. When she finally released her embrace, she had tears in her eyes. "Thank you."

"For what?"

"What you said out there, about homosexuality. I had no idea."

"You're in a big club."

She wiped her eyes. "I was wondering if maybe one day we can talk about it some more. What you said, it all went by so fast."

"Sure, let's do it. We can stretch out over a beer and take our time, instead of rushing through it. Just let me know when." Bart turned toward the sanctuary. "Listen, I've got James here. He wants to talk."

"I saw him when he came in. Go ahead. I'll catch you later."

Bart and James sat in the front row. "Listen James, before you jump all over me, I plan on apologizing to him today. I would have done it last week, but he disappeared."

"You could have called him."

"I wanted to do it in person."

"Well, just so you know, he's a mess."

"I know. I spoke to Mom last night."

"I've never seen him like this."

"Like what?"

James turned toward his brother. "Quiet as a mouse. You should have seen him at the conference. He barely said a word to anybody. People actually asked me if he was okay. At first I thought he must still be angry with you, but now, I'm beginning to wonder. He's been angry with you before, lots of times, but always got over it quick and never let it bother him. This is different. I don't know, it's not so much anger as it is grief, maybe even depression. I can't tell."

"Mom is convinced something else is going on."

James looked up at the cross. "I know. I didn't think so, but now I'm not so sure."

Bart stood. "Did you tell him I'll be coming over?"

"No. He's getting back from the conference early this evening."

"Call me when he gets in."

"You'll probably find him in the attic."

Bart frowned. "The attic? What's he doing up there?"

"Mom didn't tell you? He's been holed up in there most of the week when he's not in the church. I crawled up there one afternoon to check on him. He ordered me downstairs. When we do see him, he walks around the house with lifeless eyes, as if in a trance."

"Have you asked him what's wrong?"

"Of course I've asked him. He just brushes me off. It's so

strange. If something bothers him he usually talks our ears off about it, but now we can't get a word out of him. Poor Mom. She's a mess too. She doesn't know what to do."

Bart lowered his head. "I'll definitely see him tonight. Hopefully my apology will help."

"Make sure you tell him there's no spite in it."

"I will."

James walked over to the pulpit. "There's one other thing. Before coming over here I happened to overhear a conversation at the checkout line in Calvin's hardware store about your lecture today. Somebody must have seen all the cars and stuck their nose in. It seems a few people are pretty angry with you for continuing the lectures."

"I'm not surprised," Bart said, picking up a few scattered programs off the floor. "What did they say?"

James hesitated. "I couldn't really hear, except that it was a shame about what happened to Father, and why don't you leave, and we should do something about it, that kind of thing."

Bart froze. "—Do something about it'?"

"Yeah, I think so."

"Did they see you?"

"Yep. When they caught sight of me, they spoke louder."

Bart approached his brother and flung the programs onto the pulpit, knocking an unopened bottle of water onto the floor. "Is this your way of telling me to stop?"

"I'm sorry; I'm just reporting what I heard."

"It might have been a good time for you to jump in and defend me."

James returned the bottle to the pulpit. "You know, you may not believe this, but I almost did."

"Why didn't you?"

James pressed his lips together and lowered his head. "I'm sorry; I should have."

Bart handed the bottle back to James, retrieved another one from his knapsack, and took a large gulp. "It's probably nothing to worry about anyway."

"How is Jennifer?"

"She's fine."

"Does she know I know about her?"

Bart glanced toward the living quarters. "No."

"I guess that's best, for her sake." James took a sip. "I'll call you the moment Father gets home."

"Thanks."

James looked around the church. "You know, it's such a shame."

"What is?"

"That Father wasn't here today, to have his say, to answer questions. It would have been hard for him to sit through your lecture, but I know he would have loved to have his full say at the podium."

Bart finished his water. "Thanks for dropping by."

"I'll tell Mom you're coming over."

An hour later Bart, Sarah, and Jennifer shared a pizza, beer, and stories of their youth. Bart recounted a few funny anecdotes involving James and Junia. Sarah had them in tears with the silly shenanigans she used to pull on her two brothers in their childhood home just outside of Tel Aviv. Jennifer also had them laughing with tricks she'd played on her friends and a high school teacher. Bart sat back and smiled as the country girl from the Bible Belt in rural Alabama and the city girl from Israel shared stories of their carefree youth.

Sarah squeezed Jennifer's hand. "Hey, listen, I'm going to Israel next week for a conference. I'll be sure to bring you back a nice souvenir."

Jennifer smiled, a happy smile. "I'd like that very much. Thank you. Do you have family back there?"

Sarah hesitated. "No, but I have lots of friends. It'll be great to see them."

Through it all Bart's father never left his mind, not even for a second, but by an act of sheer will he managed to wall it off and throw it into a cortical sound-proof box, just far enough away to allow this delightful mealtime indulgence. He knew he'd be blowing the door off the hinges of that box soon enough, but for now he was happy and grateful for the ability to live in the present.

Sarah jumped up and looked around the room. "Did I leave my purse in the car? Jenn, I've got a couple of photographs I'd like to show you. I'll be back in a second."

After a few moments of silence Jennifer touched Bart's hand. "She sure is a sweetheart. If you don't mind me asking, do you two plan on—"

Sarah returned with anger in her eyes. "You're not going to believe this."

Bart jumped up. "What is it? Did you lose your purse?"

"Follow me. I've got something to show you."

They stood before the sign, smashed, lying on its side. Sarah turned to Bart. "I can't believe this is happening."

Bart began to pick up letters scattered at his feet. "Do we have enough supplies?"

"Again?"

"Again. As many times as it takes."

"Takes for what?"

"Until it stays up."

Sarah threw her hands on her hips. "Bart Trask, you are a stubborn man."

"Is that what I am?"

"Well, come on, let's get it done, before it gets dark."

"Let's first say goodnight to Jenn."

"Are you going to tell her?"

"I'll say the wind blew it over."

Ninety minutes later, after rebuilding the sign and dropping Sarah at Junia's place, Bart finally headed to the Trask home to see his father. He pulled into the driveway, opened his car door, placed one foot onto the woodchips, and fell back onto the seat. He tried to organize his scattered thoughts but got nowhere.

James met him in the driveway. "He's in the church."

Through the near darkness, illuminated only by a few dim lights lining the sanctuary, he found his father sitting in the front row, his shoulders slumped, his head bowed. For a moment Bart waited in the back. Finally, he crept down the center aisle, hesitated upon reaching the front row, then slid in next to his father. Bart placed his hands in his lap, looked at the immense wooden cross, and took a silent deep breath. For about ten minutes the two men sat in silence, the quiet broken only by the faint ticking of an invisible clock.

"Father, I'm sorry for what I said in the bedroom." Bart waited. His father said nothing. "I'm sorry I accused you of planning to sabotage the lecture. I *know* that's not true. I lost my head. I'm sorry. Please forgive me."

Theodosius turned to his son. "Thank you," he said, with a raspy voice.

"Please know that what I'm doing ... there's no spite in it. I don't want to hurt you. I can't deny that I want to be heard, perhaps by you as much as anybody else, maybe even more if I'm honest, but it's not to hurt you."

"I know," he said softly.

"James tells me you've not been yourself lately."

"No, I suppose I haven't been."

"I know the lecture must have been hard on you, but the way you left.... No matter how upset you were, it just doesn't seem like something you would do. Is anything else—"

"James tells me you're quite the speaker."

"Father, is anything else going on?"

Theodosius slowly rose and left the church, leaving Bart alone with the creaking of the walls and ticking of the invisible clock.

On the flight back to Chapel Hill the following morning, Bart couldn't stop thinking about his father's response in the church. Instead of harboring at least some degree of residual anger or even just a little righteous indignation his father had seemed, if anything, depressed, even grief stricken. Why?

After staring out into the infinite pale blue for what felt like hours, Bart lowered the blind. Could his father just be feeling terribly disappointed with himself, even guilty for leaving the lecture before getting the chance to set the audience straight? Perhaps, but knowing him, the last thing he'd do would be to fall into a terrible depression and detach himself from his family and community. He would've tripped over himself racing to the pulpit the following Sunday morning to have his say instead of giving the service to James. With a shake of his head, Bart closed his eyes, hoping for sleep.

Three nights later, while watching a movie with Sarah, Bart received a call from James.

"I'm calling about Father. He's in terrible shape."

Bart jumped off the couch. "What's going on?"

"He's hardly spoken to us. He walks around the house with such a sadness in his eyes, as if somebody in the family just died. I've never seen him like this before. I figured by this time he'd have gotten over whatever it is, but if anything he seems to be getting worse."

"Something else *must* be going on. I'll talk to him after the lecture."

"Poor Mom, she's a wreck."

"I'll talk to him, I promise. Let her know."

Bart flopped onto the couch next to Sarah. "Father is getting worse."

"What's happened?"

"I don't know. He seems to be spiraling down into some kind of terrible depression. I don't get it. He *always* bounces back. Why not now?"

—⁓—

Two days later, Sarah left for her trip to Israel. Later that day, Bart flew back to Traskville, once again arriving at Junia's place late Friday evening. He had considered calling James for a further update on their father after landing in Birmingham but decided against it. He would drop in for a visit after the lecture.

Early Saturday morning, with the warm May sun barely piercing the auroral sky, and with mother and child fast asleep, Bart headed to the church to make a few minor revisions in his presentation. He loved the absolute quiet and stillness of an empty church for work, contemplation, or just to clear his mind.

As he approached the church, his heart sank. Once again, his sign had been assaulted. Both posts had been fractured, standing as two crooked, jagged pieces of wood pointing in different directions. The new fiberglass cover, obtained from the contractor's stash of materials, had also been cracked. The letters were nowhere to be found. He gently touched one of the posts, shook his head, and headed for the church.

Upon entering the front door Bart heard music coming from the living quarters. He slowly approached. "Jenn?"

She emerged from her "she-shack," as she called it, wearing a housecoat, her hair up in a towel, a coffee mug in her hand. "Good morning!"

"Good morning! What are you doing up so early?"

She laughed. "I'm an early bird. What are you doing here so early?"

"I just thought I'd come over and work on my presentation."

"Can I get you a coffee?"

"Sure."

Bart discovered a partially completed 500-piece jigsaw puzzle on the kitchen table. "Nice! Where'd you get this?"

"I found it tucked away in a tiny drawer in the closet."

The box revealed a painting of Jesus delivering his Sermon on the Mount. Jennifer had managed to complete the border and part of Jesus's head and body. Bart dropped a puzzle piece into place. "Got one!" He looked at Jennifer and smiled, channeling his best recollection of childhood puzzle-making with his siblings and mother on the dining room table.

Jennifer handed him his coffee. "I'm glad I found it; it can get pretty boring around here."

"Do you ever go into the church?"

"All the time, but only late at night."

"How can you see?"

"I light a candle and carry it around. Don't worry; there's

no way anybody outside could see it." She dropped another piece into place. "By the way, three nights ago I think I may have had a few visitors."

Bart straightened. "You what?"

"I thought I heard some noise coming from the front of the church when I was cleaning up."

"What kind of noise?"

"I thought it was voices, but I couldn't be sure. A few minutes later, I heard a pickup truck drive off. I thought of calling you, but I figured it was just some kids, so I went to bed."

"What time did this happen?"

"I don't know exactly, about ten, I'd say."

Bart thought about his sign. "You're right, it's probably just some teenagers out for a little fun. Give me a call, anytime, if you get any more visitors, okay?"

"Sure."

He gave her a hug and crept out into the church, thinking about what James had overheard in town.

Two hours later, Bart greeted Junia and Thomas with hugs and kisses. They sat on the deck in the back and talked while the little guy played with his cars.

"They busted my sign again."

Junia's eyes grew wide. "Oh no!"

"Jennifer thinks she may have heard a couple of voices and a pickup truck three nights ago."

"Did you tell her about the sign?"

"No, I didn't want to worry her."

"If you need some help with the rebuild, just let me know."

"Thanks, but I've got it. At this point I think I can do it in my sleep."

Junia reached over and gently grasped her brother's wrist. "I've got to say, it's great to have you around. I miss my brother. I brag about you all the time."

"Brag about me? About what?"

"Oh, just that you're a professor and writing books and giving lectures and you're brilliant, and all that."

"Hey, I'm no smarter than you."

She lowered her head. "Yeah, right."

"Besides, you're accomplishing more than I could ever manage." He pointed to Thomas. "Look at that beautiful little boy you've got. You're such a great mother. It can't be easy raising a child on your own, the right way, while having to work. What I do is nothing compared to that."

"Mom helps me a lot."

"I'm telling you, it's more than I could handle."

She smiled. "Maybe, but you got something I wish I had."

"What?"

"Courage."

"What do you mean?"

Junia's eyes filled with water. "What do I mean? Look at me. A twenty-eight-year-old widow, working part-time at a warehouse distribution center in Birmingham, sponging off my parents down the street to help keep the lights on. I want to get out of here and jump back into that nursing program so bad I can't stand it, but that would take courage. So I stay."

"Oh, come on, that's not fair. You've got a child to care for. You can't just up and run, like Jennifer. I'm sorry you feel trapped; that's got to be frustrating, but don't give up hope for something better. I didn't realize you wanted to get back into nursing."

She wiped her eyes. "And then I look at you, coming here, doing your thing, doing *you* as hard as you can, knowing it ain't going to be easy. Yet you do it."

"Junia, my challenges are nothing compared to yours."

"Maybe, but it can't be easy to see Father and everybody else walk out on you like that, and to see your sign knocked down every ten minutes, and for people to be talking about you behind your back. That takes courage."

Bart sat up. "Have you heard people talking about me?"

She shook her head and waved her arm dismissively. "It's not even worth mentioning."

He leaned forward. "What did you hear?"

"I was at the hardware store last week getting a new screen door. A certain person offered his condolences to me that you were my brother. Condolences. Can you imagine? I wanted to slap the teeth right out of his drunk-ass mouth."

Bart frowned. "Who?"

Junia rolled her eyes. "Who do you think? If I were Jenn, I'd never go back."

"Did he say anything else?"

"Yeah, that you should get the hell out of town, and stay out."

Bart's eyes widened. "He said that, exactly?"

"Don't worry. He's just a drunk douchebag. He's not worth paying any attention to."

Bart paused. "I was wondering. You don't think I have some kind of anti-Christian agenda going on, do you?"

"If you mean Christian fundamentalism, for sure. Everybody knows that."

"No, I was thinking Christianity as a whole—Catholics, Protestants, the whole thing."

Junia shrugged. "I don't know. I haven't really thought about it. Why do you ask?"

Bart flopped back onto his recliner. His eyes fell onto the cloudless sky. He exhaled loudly. "I guess with everything that's happening I'm suddenly wondering if my message is as clear as I think it is. It's really not meant to be anti-Christian."

"Maybe, but I can see how people like Father and his church would have a problem with what you're saying."

"Oh, I know." Bart sat up. "Where is *your* faith these days?"

Junia shrugged. "I believe in some kind of something, I guess. I just haven't figured it out. Father gave up on my faith a long time ago."

"Does he hassle you?"

"Maybe a little, from time to time, but not much. I go to church and play the part, sort of, to keep him halfway satisfied. Now you, you're a different story."

"What do you mean?"

Junia smiled sadly. "He had such hopes and dreams for you."

"He's got James."

"I know, but … I don't know how to explain it. He's proud of James, following in his footsteps and all, but back in the day, I'm telling you, *you* were the one. The way he used to look at you.…"

Bart frowned. "I was the one? Come on, that's crazy."

"In the beginning? For sure. You were the chosen one, the one to follow in Father's footsteps. I heard him say it when we were kids. He saw something special in you."

"I guess things have changed, huh?"

"I don't know. Have they?"

Bart slid to the floor and rolled a car toward Thomas. "Would you like some company over the next few days? I'd love to hang out with you and little Thomas for a while. For a New Testament scholar, I'm rather handy with my mitts. I've got a little work to do, but I'd love to help you guys out. I can get that screen up for you, and stuff like that."

"Sure, I'd love it."

Bart stood. "I'd better get going. I've got to go into town to get some supplies to fix the sign."

"You sure you don't need any help?"

"I'll be fine, thanks. I'll see you after the lecture.

Bart headed into town with a mission. He needed to pick up some lumber for the sign, but he also wanted to sniff around to learn anything he could about what James and Junia had heard. Would anyone be bold enough to confront him to his face?

Due for a haircut, he thought he might stop in at the hair salon. As he entered the place, he immediately recognized two people who had attended his first lecture, a middle-aged, round-faced man with a well-groomed red beard waiting on his son, and Gerry Tanner, a mechanic at one of the local garages getting a trim. The bearded man's eyes widened.

"Hey, are you the one who gave that speech at the church a couple of weeks ago?"

Gerry turned toward Bart. "Surprised you're still around with the reception you got, especially from your father."

Bart smiled. "I'm still here."

The bearded man sat next to Bart. "So is that what you teach, at the University?"

"It's part of what I teach."

"Interesting. I didn't expect that at all. I like history, all sorts, really, but I never thought about … well, Bible history, as history. It almost seems kind of strange to think of the Bible in that way, you know what I mean?"

"For sure. You're not alone. A lot of folks—"

Gerry jumped out of his chair and turned to Bart. "Let me tell you, *professor*, you've got a lot of people in this town pretty upset with all this history mumbo-jumbo you're spouting off. You may be acting all innocent, but we know what you're doing."

"What would that be?"

"Stomping on your father, that's what."

"And who is 'we'?"

"I'd say you better get the hell out of town pronto, Amigo."

"Do you know who's breaking my signs?"

Gerry grinned. "What sign?"

"I'm giving a lecture this afternoon. You're welcome to come and give it another try."

"Over my dead body." Gerry gave the hairstylist a sweet smile, paid his bill, and left. The man with the red beard shrugged.

Bart sat in the salon chair. "Sorry about that."

"So you're the guy I've been hearing about."

"What have you heard?"

"Oh, something about Pastor Trask's son blowing into town and giving a speech against God."

"Please don't believe what you heard."

She shrugged. "Don't worry; all that religion stuff don't mean a lot to me. I mean I believe in God and go to church and all that, but...."

"You're not going to stab me with your scissors?"

She laughed. "No way. I need the tip. Now sit back and don't move. I don't have all day."

Bart sat in his car, his guts quivering. If he needed to know the temperature of the soup, he had already tasted enough to burn his tongue. Evidently other tongues, burning with indignation, were wagging hard and fast.

He entered the hardware store and headed for the lumber section, that all-too-familiar corner of the building he was hoping to never revisit. Out of the corner of his eye he caught a glimpse of Calvin at the cash register. His jaw tightened.

With his shopping complete—cement, posts, letters, white plastic square sign, and fiberglass cover—he headed to the cashier. He recognized the young woman immediately as someone he had frequently babysat.

"Helen? Is that you? It's Bart Trask."

Helen smiled politely while she scanned his items without looking at him.

"How are you? How are your folks?"

As if reluctantly, Helen looked at him. "Fine," she muttered. "I'm going to Alabama State this fall."

"That's fantastic! Congratulations! What are you studying?"

Calvin entered through a door from behind the counter. He glared at Bart. "Can I help you out to your car with that, sir?" He came around the counter, grabbed the cart, and headed for the door, leaving Bart standing with Helen. She pulled her eyes away from him and completed the transaction. Two customers, neither of whom he knew but thought he may have recognized from his first lecture, stared past Bart toward the cash, conspicuously indifferent.

Bart caught up with Calvin just outside the store. "I'll take it from here, thank you."

Calvin grinned. "You seem to be buying a lot of wood lately. Building something?"

"Somebody has been tearing down my sign."

"Oh, that's a crying shame."

"Calvin, is there anything else you want to say to me?"

"I'd say your daddy did all the saying that needs to be said when he left you looking pretty silly. How dare you embarrass such a fine man like that?"

Bart slammed the trunk shut. "Thanks for your help."

Calvin's eyes hardened. "Let me spell it out for you. We don't want you and your anti-God message here. You got that? You and your pointy-nosed bitch better pack up and get out of town, or else."

Bart stiffened. Jennifer flashed through his mind. The muscles in his arms tightened. The outside world, even the ground below his feet, vanished. Boiling up within him came a powerful urge to strike. He stepped back, exhaled, and smiled. "I plan on giving another lecture today. I'd invite you but unfortunately tickets are all sold out."

"I'm warning you...."

Bart sped out of the lot, cursing. He turned into the elementary school parking lot down the road, brought the rental car to a screeching halt, and pounded the wheel.

Pathetic bastard!

———❦———

As Bart pulled up to the remnants of his destroyed sign, the church caught his eye. The structure really was a relic of days long past, but there it was, leaning ever so slightly to the left. He wondered, in its long history, with all the services it had hosted, had it ever served such an important, humane role as it now did, providing safety and refuge for a frightened young woman?

While poking at the earth with a fragment of wood splintered off the fractured signpost, he spotted a droopy, defenseless dandelion at the base of the sign. He cleared fragments of wood away from it, built a little earth fence around it, and watered it from some bottled water he had in the car.

He glanced at his watch. Three hours before the lecture. With a deep sigh, he pulled himself up to his feet as if a tired old man had suddenly crawled inside his bag of skin. An hour later, soaking in sweat, with a sore left shoulder and lower back, he looked at the new sign—straight as an arrow, letters perfectly aligned and centered.

Why had he taken such care? He knew it would likely be bulldozed again. He glanced at his sad little ill-fated dandelion. He thought of his mother's roses. How she loved and cared for them. She knew they would shrivel up and die, like roses always do, but it sure didn't stop her. It's a funny thing. It's as if the dying gave greater meaning to the living. Signs, dandelions, roses, old churches, even people.

His ugly encounter with Calvin came roaring back to him. After a few minutes of failed reflection, his mind nothing more than dissonant static, he threw his tools into his trunk and headed off to Junia's place.

Bart tried to shake off his dysphoria with a scorching hot shower, a delicious lunch, and a few minutes with Thomas, but nothing seemed to help. On the way to the church, he decided to adopt a different strategy. Instead of trying to flush out all the anger and threats hurled at him, he would use it constructively. By sheer force of will, he would redouble his efforts to drop himself as deep as possible into the shoes of every fundamentalist Christian in the audience, right down to their souls, and deliver not only his tightest, cleanest performance yet, but with all the sympathy, compassion, and empathy possible. He mustn't forget that for many, he would be delivering a nightmare. Extraordinary care must be taken.

Bart strode up to the podium, looked out at the packed audience, and offered a broad smile.

"Good afternoon, folks. Welcome. Thanks for coming. I'm Bart Trask...."

As the new and improved lecture proceeded, Bart once again heard a smattering of snarls and contempt and witnessed scattered defections, but overall the lecture was well received.

Three hours later, determined not to let the disturbing

events from earlier in the day bother him, Bart sat at the kitchen table with Junia and Jennifer and tried to enjoy a beer. Upon leaving the church he checked his sign. It remained unscathed. Even his adopted dandelion seemed a little less droopy.

That evening Bart attended a barbecue at Junia's place with the entire family, including his father. They shared family stories, laughed at Junia's bad jokes, and ate too much, just like the old days. The family tried to include Theodosius in any and all light conversations, but apart from the occasional forced smile and brief comment he remained conspicuously quiet.

Amidst a facade of casual merriment, Bart could see concern on everyone's face. An invisible heaviness hung in the air. His mother tried to wear a mask of contentment, but she couldn't disguise her eyes. She tightly clutched her husband's arm and virtually never left his side. Bart considered pulling his father aside toward the end of the evening, or seeing him later, but couldn't bring himself to do it.

Soon after everyone left, Bart crawled into bed. He looked forward to spending a few days with Junia and Thomas. Tomorrow he would pay a visit to his father.

He rolled over, closed his eyes, emptied his tired mind, and waited for sleep.

"Bart! Wake up! Fire!"

Bart sprang to his feet, shattering vague dream fragments of his lecture the previous afternoon. "What? Fire? Where?"

"Outside." Junia grabbed his wrist and rushed him through the open front door onto the porch. To the southwest, flames and streaks of light shot high into the night sky. The smell of smoke filled his nostrils. Junia threw her hands up to her face. "I think it's your church!"

A jolt of electricity shot through Bart. "Jennifer! Call 911 and James. Now!"

With only pajama bottoms on, Bart ran into the house, grabbed his phone and keys, jumped into his car, and sped toward the church. A minute later, his mouth flew open. The entire church, and even his sign, were engulfed in roaring flames. With his heart pounding and his insides convulsing, he raced to the back of the church. Scorching heat and smoke poured out of the shattered back windows and door. He tried to approach the door but was kicked back by the intense heat.

"Jennifer! Can you hear me?"

Two vehicles came roaring around the side of the church, both nearly slamming into Bart's car. James, Theodosius, and

Junia jumped out. Bart turned to them. "She's in there!" He grabbed Junia by the shoulders. "Did you call 911?"

"Yes, and her father."

At that moment, Calvin Adams's truck came flying around the corner, glancing off Junia's car, smashing her left brake light. He staggered toward the door, crying out his daughter's name, but was thrust back by smoke and heat, coughing, his hands over his face. Several other trucks and cars also appeared. Sirens filled the smoke-filled night air.

Two squad cars pulled up. Bart met them as they jumped out. "A young woman is in there. Where the hell is the fire truck?"

"They're coming as fast as they can," the officer said. "They're quite a ways out."

Calvin disappeared into the smoke surrounding the door, emerging a moment later coughing and sputtering. An officer attempted to pull him away, but he broke free and crashed through the shattered door. An officer tried to follow him in but was thrown back, his eyes squeezed shut, gasping for breath.

Junia slumped to the ground, wailing. Bart could barely stand, overcome with nausea. Suddenly his head shot up. A barely audible shout from Jennifer could be heard. James approached the door, recoiled, then dove in again, but this time didn't reappear. Junia leaped to her feet and shrieked. The front section of the church collapsed. Bart lunged toward the door but was repelled by billows of thick smoke. An officer grabbed him by the bare arm and threw him onto the grass.

Fifteen seconds later, just as a firetruck and two EMS units arrived with sirens screaming, James suddenly emerged, eyes shut tight, coughing and wheezing, with Jennifer in his arms. He staggered onto the uneven ground and fell forward, dumping her onto the grass, partially landing on her. She lay on her back, her extremities limp, her eyes closed.

"She's not breathing!" Junia screamed.

Two paramedics descended on her and began resuscitation. A third attended to James as he sat in the grass sputtering and wheezing. "Her father ... he's in there," he managed to say in a croaking voice between fits of coughing.

With tear-filled eyes, Bart stared at Jennifer's limp, motionless body.

Powerful streams of water from two high pressure hoses shot into the living quarters. Two firemen immediately burst in through what little remained of the back door. Paramedics placed a breathing tube into Jennifer's lungs and mechanically ventilated her. Her face, arms, and legs appeared covered in soot. James, coughing madly, grimacing, and moaning, was given oxygen by a mask. A section in the middle of the church came crashing down. More sirens filled the air. The paramedics transferred James into an ambulance and sped away, sirens blazing.

The firemen emerged, one of them carrying Calvin on his back. They laid him out on the grass. His lifeless face, and most of the rest of him, was scorched and soaking. He wasn't breathing. A paramedic began cardiopulmonary resuscitation. No response. He was pronounced dead at 3:27 a.m.

A helicopter could suddenly be heard. A few moments later the air-ambulance, gleaming blue and white with red trim and the words MedEvac written on the side above the door, landed at the back of the church. Within seconds the flight paramedic and nurse loaded Jennifer into the ambulance and, with a ferocious gust of wind, disappeared into the night sky.

Bart approached one of the paramedics. "Where are they taking them?"

"UAB Trauma Center Burn Unit."

He grabbed Junia's hand. "They're headed to UAB. Come on; I'll take you."

"Are you sure you can drive? You can barely stand."

"Come on, let's go."

Bart found his father sitting in his car, eyes flared, gripping the steering wheel with both hands. Bart threw open the door.

"Are you okay?" Theodosius didn't respond. "They're taking them to UAB. We'll take you."

He shook his head.

"Are you sure?"

Theodosius's face tightened. "The police found a couple of gas cans at the side of the church."

Bart sped to Birmingham with the windows down and radio off. With the wind howling in his ears, the blinding lights of oncoming trucks, and tears streaming down his cheeks, all he could hear were the warnings of James, Junia, the man in the barbershop, and Calvin. All he could see was his sign—destroyed, repaired, and destroyed again—and most of all poor unsuspecting Jenn, in her house coat, smiling, doing a crossword puzzle, lying half-dead in the grass.

Junia touched him on the arm. He pulled away. She

grabbed his arm again, this time hanging on. "She's young, she's going to make it."

"I should have got her out of there. I should have seen this coming. I tried to help her, but I ended up...."

"Bart, there's no way on earth you could have known this was coming."

"I can't stop seeing her face, lying there in the grass, not breathing."

"She's not going to die. She's going to fight. She's going to survive."

They arrived several minutes later. Bart sprinted into the ER. "We're looking for Jennifer Adams and James Trask."

"They both just got transferred to the Burn Unit."

A nurse from the Burn Unit escorted them into the empty waiting room. "Please, have a seat."

Bart remained standing. "How are they?"

"Your brother has got some burns on his arms and face, and a little smoke inhalation, but he's going be okay. We're going to keep him here for observation."

His stomach tightened. "What about Jennifer?"

The nurse hesitated.

Oh no ... please ... no....

"She's still with us, thanks to the EMS guys. She's minimally responsive, on a ventilator. She's also got some superficial burns but it's mostly smoke inhalation."

"Can we see them?"

They entered James's room. His face and arms were bandaged. An IV hung at the bedside. He wore an oxygen mask. A monitor on a shiny metal pole beeped and flashed. Bart gently touched his brother's hand. "How are you feeling?"

James grimaced. "Pain. Tough to breathe," he whispered.

Junia touched his cheek. "You're a hero, my brother."

"Jennifer. Is she...."

"She's here. They flew her in by helicopter. They're working on her."

James closed his eyes. A nurse came in. "I'm going to ask you to step out. Your brother needs his rest."

They entered Jennifer's room. Bart laid eyes on her and gasped. There she lay, intubated, ventilated, her arms wrapped in gauze. Multiple tubes, IV bags, and pumps, all beeping and flashing, surrounded her. His eyes filled with fresh tears. Junia took him by the arm and led him out to the waiting room. They sat, heads lowered, silent, motionless. Bart thought of Sarah. How he wished she were here, next to him. He glanced at his watch, calculated the time in Israel to be late morning, and pulled out his phone.

"Hello, sweet man. You're up awfully early."

"I wish I wasn't," he said in a raspy monotone.

"Honey, what's wrong? Are you okay? What happened?"

Barely able to push out the words, Bart revealed the harrowing events of the evening.

"Sarah, I should have plucked her out of there when I had the chance. I should have—"

"Bart, hang on, please listen to me. Whatever happens—"

"She may die! Do you hear that?"

"Believe me, I do hear it, my love. I know there's nothing I can say now that's going to make you feel better, but whatever happens to Jenn, you're going to feel ripped to shreds and horribly guilty for a long while, because that's how you're made, but here's the thing...."

Junia gently placed her hand on Bart's shoulder. He pulled away. "Sarah, please don't try to—"

"Listen to me! In the fullness of time you will slowly begin to realize, and then feel it in your bones, that you're not to blame for this terrible thing. Slowly but surely you're going to accept that neither you, nor anyone else in your shoes, could have or should have foreseen this terrible tragedy. You know why you're going to realize that? Because it's the truth. I know this doesn't help you now, but I *promise* you, you'll get there, with me right by your side, with all the love and help I can give you. I'll be back in ten short days."

Theodosius suddenly burst into the waiting room, followed by Linda. Bart's eyes widened. "My parents just arrived. I've got to go." He jumped up. "Have you seen them?"

Theodosius stared at his son, or rather through him, his eyes wet with tears. His mother clung to his arm, her face contorted with grief. Bart escorted them to chairs. "James is going to be okay."

Theodosius slowly lifted his head. "Is Jennifer going to survive?"

Bart hesitated. "We don't know yet."

Junia took her father's hand. "She's young and strong. She's going to make it."

Theodosius looked up at the ceiling and grimaced. He wiped his eyes, leaned forward, and hung his head down. The light from a dim bulb in the corner of the small room fell upon the side of his face. "Can you ladies please step out for a moment? I need to speak to Bartholomew."

Bart sat next to his father. After several minutes of silence, broken only by the muffled machine sounds from the burn

unit, Theodosius took a deep breath. "I didn't think for a second that…." He shook his head.

Bart frowned. "What?" He sprang to his feet. "What did
you just say?"

"It was just talk."

"What talk? Did you … know something … about the
fire?"

Theodosius lowered his head.

Bart's eyes widened. "You knew about the fire?"

"No."

"Then what are you saying?"

"Old Jacobs pulled me aside last Sunday after church. He
told me he overheard Calvin talking about you the day before,
just after you gave your second lecture. Jacobs claims Calvin
said if you continued, something would have to be done to
stop you, 'one way or the other.'"

"Calvin said that—one way or the other?"

"Yes."

Bart threw his hands in the air. "Why the hell didn't you
tell me?"

Theodosius looked at his son with wet eyes. "I didn't think
he was going to do anything, at least nothing like this."

"You actually thought he might do something?"

"No! I don't know. Maybe just a protest. As God is my
witness, I didn't think for a second something like this could
happen." Theodosius lowered his head and covered his eyes.
"Dear God, what have I done!"

His father's failure to warn him had instantly boiled Bart's
insides, but this anger, this flare of righteous indignation, so
perversely comforting if only for a microsecond, immediately

shamed him. He swung his chair directly in front of his father, sat, and gently placed his hand on his father's knee. "I'm sorry. You're right. You couldn't have imagined this. The truth is, I heard things too, and was told things directly to my face, and I did nothing. And *I* knew Jenn was in the church."

"I should have said something to you," Theodosius muttered.

"Father, I'm telling you, it wouldn't have made any difference."

Theodosius looked up. "Why was she there?"

Bart hesitated. The obvious question caught him off guard. "She was just helping me to finish up a few odd jobs and … uh, acting as kind of temporary custodian." He leaned forward until what little space between them nearly vanished. "Father, she was my responsibility. I should have protected her, and I didn't. This is on me, not you."

Theodosius shook his head. "It's not just that I kept my mouth shut."

"What do you mean?"

"Where do you think he got the idea?"

"Father, you didn't tell him to burn the church down."

"No, but tell me this—do you think it would have happened if I hadn't left the lecture?"

Theodosius pushed himself up to his feet, wiped his eyes, and left the room.

Late the following morning, Bart sat at Jennifer's bedside. A few hours of fitful sleep did little to decrease his shock and grief at her appearance—flat on her back, on a ventilator, eyes closed, surrounded by beeping monitors, flashing numbers, and wiggly lines. A doctor entered the room, examined her, and looked at the monitors.

"Doc, how is she doing?"

"A little better."

He exhaled. "That's great. How long is she going to need the breathing tube?"

"It's hard to say. We may be able to start weaning her off the vent within the next day or two if all goes well."

"Could something bad happen?"

"Sure. She could develop pneumonia or not continue to recover as fast."

"When is she going to wake up?"

"She was a wee bit frisky with the tube in there. We've increased her sedation a little until we're ready to dial down the vent."

"That's a good thing, isn't it, that she's frisky?"

"Yes, it is. It tells us her brain is active, but we're going to have to wait and see."

Bart looked away. "We thought we lost her."

"I'd say she came pretty close. If your brother hadn't plucked her out of there when he did, she wouldn't have made it."

Bart kissed Jennifer on her bandaged hand and left.

———

He found James sitting in a recliner in the sunroom, reading. "Hey, look at you! How do you feel?"

James smiled, then grimaced.

"You okay?"

"Yeah. It just hurts from the burn on my neck."

Bart pulled up a chair and sat facing his brother. He glanced at the bandages over his neck, forearms, and left lower shin. "How's the breathing?"

"Okay. I'm still coughing, but the doc says I'll have that for a while."

"When are you going home?"

"As soon as I get my prescriptions." James coughed, a dry hacking bark, causing him to wince. "Mom is on her way. I didn't know you were coming. How is Jennifer?"

"The doc said she's coming along. They should be removing the breathing tube sometime over the next couple of days."

"That's just great. I've never prayed so much in all my life. I saw her early this morning."

"The doc said if you hadn't pulled her out of there…. You saved her life."

James adjusted himself in his chair and grimaced. "I just hope she's okay." He paused. "Listen, there's something I need to tell you. When we pulled up, I thought I smelled a whiff of gasoline, like in the grass."

Bart glanced toward the door, pulled his chair toward his brother until their knees touched, and locked onto his eyes. "The police found gas cans next to the church."

For a moment, James sat motionless, his eyes wide, blinking rapidly, staring past his brother. He shook his head and opened his mouth, as if to coax out the word. "Arson? I can't even imagine—" A series of violent, dry coughs bent him forward in his chair. "I know some people were upset with you, but to burn down the place?"

Bart walked over to the window and stared blankly into the parking lot. "It looks like I did a great job keeping Jenn safe, didn't I?"

"You think this was your fault?"

Bart turned toward his brother. "Come on, James, the warning signs were screaming at me. What did I do? Nothing! Instead of pulling poor Jenn out of there, I turned my back on her."

"Don't be ridiculous. There's no way you could have foreseen something like this."

"James, she had no idea. She thought she was perfectly safe. I should have told her."

"Bart, listen to me. *I* knew she was in there. Junia did too. And Sarah. We knew how people were feeling, but it never occurred to me for a second that she could actually be in danger. If I thought so I would have told you. Believe me, if Junia or Sarah were concerned, they would have told you too."

"Yeah, well, you didn't speak to Adams, did you?"

"We didn't need to. We knew there was anger in the air, and we did nothing."

"It was *my* place. She was *my* responsibility. *I* promised to keep her safe."

James sat up. "I'm telling you, there's no way anyone could have suspected this."

"Would you mind saying that to Father?"

James frowned. "Why?"

Bart walked over to a bookshelf, gave a disinterested glance at the titles, and returned to his chair. "I'm not the only one who's been feeling guilty. Last night in the waiting room he confessed to me he'd heard that Adams was threatening to stop me. He feels terrible for not telling me. I'm ashamed to say I got angry with him, again, despite being threatened directly by the man himself, knowing Jenn was there, and doing nothing about it. I immediately apologized and begged him not to blame himself, but it didn't help."

James shook his head. "As if he doesn't already feel bad enough, now this. How much more can he take?"

"Now, more than ever, we've got to help him."

James coughed until his eyes watered. "I'll talk to him about the fire. I'll tell him we all knew about the threats. That should make him feel better."

"I wish it were that easy."

"What do you mean?"

"It's not just about what he overheard. He's also convinced he stoked the anger that led to the fire by storming out of the lecture."

"He said that?"

Bart waited for another series of hacking coughs to sub-side. "Yes, just before he left, before I could say a word."

"That explains a lot. Mom says after you left the ICU last night, he sat next to Jennifer with tears in his eyes for over an hour. He barely made it through church service this morning."

Their mother entered the room. "Hello boys. How is Jennifer?"

Bart stood. "Improving. The doc said if she continues to get better they should have the tube out soon."

"Thank God. Father is taking this real hard."

"I know. We talked last night."

"He was already terribly depressed. Now he's acting as if he burned down the place himself. I just wish he'd talk to me."

Bart grasped his mother's hand. "He will. Just give him a little time."

Early the following morning, Bart received a call from an arson investigator. That afternoon, they sat on Junia's back porch. After a series of preliminary questions regarding who Bart was and his connection with the church and Jennifer, the investigator, a middle-aged stocky man with jet-black hair that conspicuously contrasted with his patchy white beard, pulled out his pen and notepad.

"So, just for the record, do you know anybody who might want to burn down the church?"

"I do, actually."

The investigator raised his eyebrows. "Really? Do tell, please."

An hour later, Bart escorted the investigator back to his car and watched him drive off.

———∞———

Two days later, encouraged by favorable daily updates from the nursing staff, Bart and James visited Jennifer. Her lungs had continued to improve, permitting removal of the breathing tube that morning. They found her sitting on a bed-side chair. Bart greeted her with a smile. "Hey there. You're looking great! How do you feel?"

She coughed. "I don't really know. Better, I guess. At least that's what they say. I got a sore throat. My breathing is not so great. My burns hurt like hell. But hey, I'm alive." She turned to James. "They just told me what happened." Her eyes filled with tears. "You saved my life."

Bart wrapped his arm around his brother's shoulder. "Yes, he did."

Jennifer wiped her eyes. "It's a strange feeling, to know I almost died." She forced a smile. "To think, I hated you for rushing out of the church like that, and it's you who came rushing back in to save me."

James took her hand and smiled warmly. "I'm glad you're going to be okay."

Her smile vanished. "They told me about my father."

Bart glanced at his brother. "We're sorry."

James shook his head. "I heard him in there, Jennifer, but I couldn't see him, and I had my hands filled with you. I'm so sorry."

"I know it's a terrible thing to say, but even though he went in there after me, I don't even feel sad. I'm glad he's gone. He can't get drunk and yell at me and hit me anymore."

Bart and James grabbed chairs from across the room and sat facing her. After a few moments of silence, she turned to Bart. "Sometime last night, after the place got real quiet, your father came to visit me. It's a bit of a jumble in my head, kind of like a dream—I still had the tube in—but I could hear his voice, far off, like in the distance. I couldn't make it all out, but at one point I heard him say the words 'sorry' and 'please forgive me.' He said it over and over. Why would he say that?"

James frowned. "He came here last night? Are you sure?"

"Yes, I'm sure. He sat right next to my bed. It's almost like he was apologizing for the fire." She began to cough and wheeze, a dry hacking cough.

Bart jumped up. "I'll get the nurse."

She shook her head, breathed in some oxygen from a mask hanging on her chair, retrieved an inhaler from her bedside table, and administered two puffs. A few seconds later, her breathing improved. "I just don't get it. What was he doing next to my bed, saying these things? I know he was angry about the lectures, but I can't imagine.... Did he say anything to you about the fire?"

Bart stiffened. He hadn't been prepared for this. Had his father intended Jennifer to actually hear his bedside confession? Bart felt the weight of her eyes on him. He stood and walked over to the window. "No, he hasn't said a thing."

"Then why did he say that to me?"

"I don't know, Jenn."

"What happened anyway? What caused the fire?"

Bart hesitated. "We're not sure, but I'm afraid it looks like arson."

Jennifer's eyes widened. "What? Somebody burned down the church? Who? Why? How do you know that?"

Bart returned to his chair. "James smelled gasoline in the grass. The police found gas cans next to the church. An arson inspector paid me a visit a couple of days ago. I'm sure he'll be giving you a call soon."

Jennifer threw a hand up to her mouth. "Oh my God." With some effort, she pushed herself up in her chair. "I need to talk to your father."

Bart stood. "Jenn, it wasn't him, I promise you."

"I'm not saying it was, but it sure as hell sounds like he knows something. Why was he apologizing to me? I need to talk to your father, ASAP. Please ask him to come and see me. I need to know what he knows."

A nurse came in. "How are you feeling, sweetheart? Gentlemen, you're going to have to excuse us." She glanced at the bandages. "Time for a dressing change."

At noon the following day Bart pulled into his parents' place. His mother sat at the dining room table paying bills. She greeted him with a forced smile. "Lunch will be ready in fifteen minutes."

"Where's Father?"

"In the church."

"How's he doing?"

"Worse than ever." Linda lowered her head. "First the lecture, now this. When I look in his eyes … it's awful. It's as if he lit the match himself."

"I'll see if I can drag him in to lunch."

As Bart crept toward the church, his stomach tightened. Theodosius sat in the back row with his head bowed. Bart slid in next to him.

"Mom is worried about you. We all are."

"I'll be alright," he muttered.

"Can I talk to you for a minute, please?"

"It's almost time for lunch."

"Jennifer is going to be okay. The tube is out. She's sore and has some breathing issues, but overall, she's doing well. She's going to be just fine."

"James told me. Praise God," he said impassively.

"Father, I'm so sorry I got upset with you, again. I had no right. You may have heard things, but like I said, I heard it directly from Adams himself, straight to my face, and *I* knew Jennifer was in there. It's my fault, not yours."

Bart waited for a response, an expression, an emotion of any kind. None came. "Father, do you hear me?"

"I should have told you, warned you, insisted you take measures. I'm your father. You're my son."

"I'm a grown man, just like you."

Theodosius stood. "Lunch is ready."

"I understand you saw her two nights ago."

"I did."

"Can I ask you what you said to her?"

"Why?"

"She told James and me that she heard you speaking to her, saying you were sorry, and asking for forgiveness."

Theodosius's face tightened. He sat. "I thought she was asleep."

"She was sedated, but she could still hear at least some of what you said."

"I was praying to God, begging for His forgiveness, for what I did, and didn't do, before the fire. I didn't think she could hear me."

"She thinks you were apologizing to *her*. She wants to know for what."

"Does she know it's arson?"

"Yes."

Theodosius closed his eyes. "She thinks I had something to do with the fire?"

"I don't know. She wants to talk to you, ASAP."

"What have you told her?"

"Nothing."

After a moment of silence, Theodosius ran his fingers through his hair and took a deep breath. "I'll go see her this afternoon."

"What are you going to tell her?"

"The only thing I can. The truth."

"The truth? You're going to mention her father?"

Theodosius turned his head away.

"Father, you can't do that. Believe me, I'm not trying to protect him. If it were anybody but Jennifer, I'd blow the whistle on that bastard in a second. It's just … well, it's bad enough she almost died. Imagine how she'll feel if she thinks her own father lit the match."

"I would never say that."

"You don't have to. When you tell her he's been threatening to stop me, 'or else,' she'll *think* he did it, or at least was involved. That's like dropping a bomb on her while she's still recovering. Just say you heard some threats and leave it at that."

"And when she asks who made those threats, what do I say then—I don't know? I'm sorry, Bartholomew, but I'm not going to lie to her."

"Oh, I see, so you've never lied before, is that it?"

Theodosius stood. "I don't need to hear this."

Bart jumped up. "Remember a couple of years ago when Mom was diagnosed with a thyroid condition, and she gained all that weight before slimming down? Remember when she asked you how she looked in her pretty new dress, designed for a slender woman twenty years younger? Remember what you said to her with a loving smile? It's not what you said to me later."

"That's not the same thing at all."

"It's exactly the same thing."

"She's going to find out anyway. It's all going to come out in the arson investigation."

"Maybe, but it doesn't have to be from us, while she's still in the hospital recovering."

Theodosius looked at the cross. "I can't make any promises."

"Can I go with you to see her?"

"Do you promise to be quiet and not interfere, in any way?"

"Quiet as a church mouse. I promise."

Theodosius brushed past his son. "Come, we mustn't keep your mother waiting. We'll head out after lunch."

Bart lightly tapped on Jennifer's door.

"Come in."

They found her lying in bed watching television. Her shins, right thigh, forearms, forehead, and left cheek were all covered in bandages. She turned off the TV, glanced at Theodosius, and greeted Bart with a pensive smile. Bart placed a small vase of flowers on her bedside table. "How are you, Jenn?"

Her eyes lit up. "Thank you. They're beautiful. Still coughing, but my breathing is coming along."

"How is the pain?"

"Dressing changes are bad. They give me pain meds, but not enough."

"How long are you going to be in the hospital?"

"I'm going home tomorrow, if they can get a nurse fixed up to help me with my burns."

"Do you need a ride?"

She smiled. "That would be great."

"Consider it done. Just call me when you're ready."

Jennifer turned to Theodosius. "Thank you for coming."

Theodosius nodded. "I'm glad you're doing better."

They sat at the side of the bed, to her right. After a few

moments of awkward silence, Theodosius cleared his throat. "Bart said you wanted to speak to me."

She turned toward the window for a moment, then back to Theodosius. "It's about when you visited me a couple of nights ago. I was half asleep, but I could hear you talking to me. I couldn't make out most of the words, but I did hear you say 'I'm sorry,' and 'please forgive me,' over and over, clear as day. It didn't make any sense to me, but then I got to thinking and wondering … why were you saying that to me?"

Bart knew it was coming, but the simple question, asked without emotion, stiffened every muscle in his body. After several moments of silence, Theodosius again cleared his throat. "I was praying to God. I was confessing to him."

"Confessing to God? It sure sounded like you were talking to me. Why were you in my room, sitting next to my bed, confessing to God?"

Theodosius opened his mouth as if to answer, then closed it. He stood and walked toward the window, took a deep breath, and turned to her. "I knew absolutely nothing about the fire. If I had heard about it, I would have notified Bart and done all I could to stop it."

"Did you know I was hiding in there?"

"No."

"Then what were you confessing to God about? I'd say it was none of my business, except you were sitting right next to me. You could have done your confessing anywhere else, but you didn't. Seeing as I almost died, I'd say I deserve to know."

"I'm afraid I'm not able to share that sacred space with you."

"I'm sorry, Pastor Theo, but that's just not good enough.

You were sitting next to me confessing to God after somebody burned down the church. Why?"

Theodosius looked out the window. A few moments later, he slowly nodded. "You're right," he said, "it does have something to do with you." He returned to his seat. "I had nothing to do with the fire itself—I knew nothing about it—but I feel I'm responsible for what happened."

"Why?"

"Because I created the anger that led to the fire when I walked out of the lecture."

Jennifer furrowed her brow. She opened her mouth to speak but hesitated. "Yeah, okay, maybe, but what they did about it, the fire, that's not your fault."

"It wouldn't have happened if I hadn't left."

"It still doesn't make it your fault. The people who burned it down, it's their fault." She lowered her head. "Just so you know, I didn't think for a second you did it, being a man of God, and all that. I just couldn't figure out why you were praying over me. I'm glad you told me. I'm sorry I had to ask, Pastor Theo."

Theodosius nodded. "It's okay," he said softly.

Jennifer's face suddenly hardened. Bart waited. She said nothing.

"What is it, Jenn?"

She opened her mouth to speak, then closed it. Her eyes welled up with tears. "It just hit me. I bet I know who did it. I bet I know who lit the match. I should have thought of it before. The same guy with the gas cans at home. The same guy who burned down our shed in the backyard that stored some of my mother's paintings when she threw out all the booze. The same guy who told me he thought of burning down our house to get the insurance money. It would be just like him and his dimwitted stooges. He wasn't happy unless he was tearing someone or something down." She shook her head in disgust. "You want to know the worst of it? He's the reason I was hiding out there in the first place."

Theodosius glanced at Bart. "What do you mean? I thought—"

"He beat me up."

"Beat you up? Why?"

"He was drunk, of course, but this time there was another reason."

"What reason?"

Jennifer looked directly at Theodosius with piercing eyes. "Because I'm a lesbian."

Theodosius sat bolt upright. His face flushed.

"I know you don't approve, but I'm not going to hide who I am, not from you, or anyone, not anymore."

After several moments of silence, Bart stood. "I ... we'd better get going."

Theodosius rose slowly. He turned to Jennifer and forced a barely noticeable mouth-only smile. "I'm sorry for my part in this."

"Don't feel bad. I told you. You're not to blame."

Bart kissed her on the cheek. "I'll talk to you soon."

Theodosius shuffled through the hospital, his shoulders slumped, his head lowered. In the parking lot, Bart placed his hand on his father's shoulder. "Are you okay?" Theodosius said nothing. He pulled ahead of his son and got into the passenger side of his car. Bart stopped. What in the world was he doing? Bart couldn't remember ever driving his father any-where. He slid behind the wheel and started the car. Theodo-sius stared straight ahead with unfocused eyes.

"Father, are you sure you're okay?"

"I'm okay," he murmured.

Bart touched his father's thigh. "Is it about Jenn being a lesbian? Has that upset you?"

Theodosius turned his head toward the passenger side window.

They drove home in silence.

Bart gently eased Jennifer into the front seat of his sedan as if she were a frail, elderly woman. Her bag of supplies, thrown into the back seat, seemed to contain enough gauze and other bandages to mummify her.

She smiled brightly. "Thanks for picking me up."

"You're very welcome. It's the least I can do."

"The least you can do? Why do you say that?"

"I promised to keep you safe. You almost died."

Jennifer gave a dismissive wave. "Oh, come on, that's ridiculous."

Bart flashed back to his confrontation with Calvin Adams. He replayed the terrible threat, spoken in anger, straight to his face. A rush of warmth came over him.

"Can you stop at a pharmacy on the way? I have to pick up some medicine."

"Of course. You going to be okay at home alone?"

Jennifer's eyes narrowed. "Okay doesn't even come close. I can't wait. No one to hide from. No one to beat me up."

"When is your aunt coming in?"

"Tomorrow. I can't wait to see her."

"Did you come out to her?"

She nodded. "I sure did, right off the bat. You know what

she said? 'Good for you. It's important to be yourself.' You know what else she said? 'Mom would have said the same thing.'"

"It sounds like your mother was a special woman."

Jennifer looked out the side window. "I miss her more than I can say."

"When does Tracy get back?"

"Thirty-one days. I'm counting the minutes."

For the next fifteen miles, they drove in silence, Bart wincing with Jennifer whenever they hit a bump. About halfway home, Jennifer turned to him. "Do you think it's strange I'm glad he's gone?"

"No," Bart said without hesitation.

"Good. It does make me angry, though."

"Why?"

"When Mom died—she got brain cancer two years ago—I cried my eyes out. I've seen a few other mothers and fathers die around here. It's always the same—kids crying their eyes out. It's terrible, but, in a sad kind of way, it's the way it should be, you know? The grieving, and all that. It's a way out. But with me and him, the way I felt when I left, the way I feel now ... there ain't no healing in that."

Bart gently grasped her hand. "I'm so sorry, Jenn."

"I sure am glad you're not mad at me for what I asked your father. At least you don't seem to be."

"Of course not. I've got to say, though, I am a little surprised you told him you were a lesbian."

Jennifer's eyes widened. "Me too. It just came out. Did you see the look on his face? He turned red as a beet."

"He'll be okay. He's still going through a rough time with

the lecture, and now the fire. He's probably never actually met somebody like you, that's all. I've got to say, though, it did seem to knock him for a loop—I actually had to drive him home—but I'm sure he's already over it. After all, whether he likes it or not, he does live in the real world with the rest of us. I'm glad you told him."

"Yeah, well, with all that happened, it's about time I started telling the truth about who I am."

Bart smiled. "I couldn't agree with you more."

Jennifer looked out the side window. "I wonder, though…."

"What?"

"Never mind."

"What? Tell me."

"Now that he knows, I wonder if he still feels as guilty about what happened to me?"

"Of course he does. Believe me, I know him. He may consider it a sin, but that doesn't change his concern for you as a fellow human being one bit."

"Good to know. I'm so glad I got that business about the confession cleared up. It wasn't easy to ask him, but I just needed to know the truth."

"Yes, of course." Bart's confrontation with her father again came rushing back to him. His jaw tightened. He turned on the radio.

———

Bart found his mother in her flower garden on her knees, pruning, watering, and pulling weeds. "Where's Father? I can't find him."

Linda straightened, wiped her brow with her forearm,

and glanced uneasily up toward the roof of the house. "He's in the attic."

"Again?"

"He's been up there almost the whole time since he got home yesterday from the hospital."

"Why?"

She hovered over her azaleas, forcefully yanked a weed as if she were pulling her hand out of a dog's mouth, sending rich dark earth flying over Bart's head, and sighed loudly. "I have no idea. He won't say."

"I'll go see him."

She carelessly flung a small collection of weeds into an already full wicker basket. "He asked to be left alone."

Bart ascended the steep and narrow wooden stairs leading up to the attic. Theodosius sat in the far end on an old straight-back wooden chair next to a bookshelf packed with books, magazines, and photo albums. The smell of ancient wood and paper and dust hit Bart's nose, astonishing him for its familiarity from many years ago when he would come up here to play with James and Junia. If he had been placed in a dark room on another continent and presented with that identical smell, he would have instantly identified the source.

A single, bare light bulb hung from the apex of the V-shaped roof in the middle of the room. That poor socket had frequently been the focus of their slingshot play. Much to the consternation of the boys, Junia had almost invariably been the best shot, hitting the bulb the most often with whatever tiny ammunition they could find. How delighted they were when any one of them hit that bulb, causing it to swing like the pendulum of a grandfather clock.

Of course, on occasion the bulb exploded, sending tiny shards of glass flying into the sudden pitch blackness. That's when they would bring into action their other favorite toy— their collection of Bic lighters that Junia had found in church when cleaning the pews. With the faint glow to guide them, they would stumble around as if they had been trapped in a haunted museum, giggling to themselves, quietly shrieking in horror as if encountering some life-threatening ghost or goblin, all the while pulverizing the broken glass with their leather slippers.

Eventually, one of them would lift the trapdoor, introducing light from below and extinguishing their delightful make-believe. Fortunately, with a church in their backyard, they had access to an endless supply of lightbulbs of all shapes and sizes. And so, before dinner, they would clean up the mess and replace the bulb with the help of a stepladder with no one the wiser. It's a wonder one of them didn't cut themselves or fall and break a bone. Bart could still remember with fondness one fine summer day when their mother mentioned that the supply of bulbs seemed to be dwindling unusually fast.

Triggered by a single sniff and a brief glance, all this flooded through Bart's mind in a tsunami of recollection. In that moment, he wished they were all back there once again as children, when all that mattered was who could hit the bulb and what scary adventure lay before them, when what you "believed" and what you "knew" about the world didn't matter a lick. At that very second, he would have relinquished his PhD to revisit those golden days, even if only just once.

Bart glanced at the assortment of old boxes and stacks of clothing, magazines, books, and various other items lining both sides, wedged into where the wood struts met the floor. Theodosius slowly lifted his head until he found his son's eyes. He snapped closed a photo album sitting in his lap and looked away. Bart grabbed a straight-backed wooden chair and sat directly before him. "What in the world are you doing up here? You look terrible."

"I'm okay."

"No you're not. Mom tells me you crawled up here yesterday after seeing Jenn. Why?"

Theodosius said nothing.

"I don't understand. From where I was sitting, it seemed to go pretty well, for both of you. You answered her questions without having to lie. She didn't blame you. She even told you it wasn't your fault. Are you upset that you didn't tell her everything?"

"No."

"Are you sure it's not about her being a lesbian? You seemed to be shocked when you heard the news."

Theodosius forced a lifeless smile. "Tell your mother I'll be okay."

"I'll tell her if you give me a reason to believe it." Bart glanced at the leather binder on his father's lap. "What are you looking at?"

"Photos."

"Of whom?"

Theodosius hesitated. "Thank you for coming to check on me."

Bart fell back in his chair. A few moments later, he pushed himself up. "Okay then, I'll leave you alone."

On the way out he tapped the bulb.

For the next several days, Bart threw his energies into helping Junia with a few small home projects, doing university work, musing over an idea for a new book on Christianity in American politics, and his favorite thing—playing with Thomas. Through all this, his thoughts were never far from recent events. He called Jennifer for an update. She was doing well. He spoke at length with Sarah. From a friend's condo in Tel Aviv, she patiently listened to his rambling ruminations, offering her love and support, and promised to be back in Chapel Hill late the following evening. On two occasions he pulled up his parent's home phone number, hovered over the call icon, and backed out. His father wanted to be left alone. Bart would leave him alone, at least for now.

The following morning, he met once again with the arson investigator at Junia's place. After answering several additional questions about himself, his family, Jennifer, and Calvin Adams, Bart tried to ask a few questions of his own, but got no answers other than confirmation that the fire was indeed a case of arson and that Bart would be apprised of the ongoing investigation as information came to light. After the visit he called Pastor Stafford to again offer his deepest apologies and give him a further update.

Shortly after speaking to Stafford, he received a call from James.

"Are you still in town?"

"Yep."

"Father wants to speak to us. Can you and Junia come over?"

"I'm putting us on speakerphone. Junia's here. What's going on?"

"I have no idea. He spends most of his time in the church or the attic. He looks white as a sheet. He seems to have taken yet another tailspin since he last saw Jennifer. Now he's barely eating. Mom is worried sick. She's beginning to wonder if he's got some terrible disease. I just don't get it. First the lecture, then the fire, and now Jennifer."

"Has he said anything to Mom?"

"About what's going on with him? Not a word."

"When does he want to see us?"

"Now, if possible, or as soon as you can. He's up in the attic."

Bart looked at Junia. She nodded. "We'll be right over."

—⟡—

Theodosius sat in his chair next to the bookshelf, his head lowered, his hands resting on a photo album in his lap. He pointed to the straight-backed wooden chairs placed in a semicircle before him. "Please, sit down."

Bart sat to his father's left, Junia in the middle, James to his right. After staring with unfocused eyes at the shiny leather album cover for several moments, Theodosius opened the album, extracted a photograph, and handed it to Bart.

Bart glanced at the photo. "Who is that?" He handed it to Junia.

"My brother, Thaddeus."

Theodosius took the photo back from James and carefully replaced it in its faded plastic envelope. "I took that picture the year he died." He paused. "One summer afternoon, on the way home from seminary, we stopped for ice cream. He seemed troubled. I asked him if everything was okay. He said no, he had something to tell me."

The trees rustled in the breeze. The wooden floor creaked. A dull electrical hum from the house below filled the silence.

"He told me...." Theodosius shut his eyes and bowed his head. A moment later he slowly lifted his head and found Bart's eyes. "He told me he was a homosexual."

Bart's eyes sprang wide open. "What?"

"He confessed he'd wanted to tell me for a long time, but he could never bring himself to do it. He was terrified of people finding out, especially Father and people at seminary, but he just couldn't hold it in anymore. He said he had to tell somebody, and that somebody was me."

"What did you say? I mean, how did you react?"

"I was shocked, of course. I just sat there, stunned. He looked at me with such misery in his eyes, waiting for me to say something. I asked him if he knew what scripture said about homosexuality. He said he did. I told him that's all he needed to know. I suggested he step away from seminary and seek help from Exodus, the Christian organization to help people who have homosexual desires, to find his way back to God's grace. I told him I loved him, God loved him, and I would pray for him."

Bart stiffened. He suddenly felt a powerful compulsion to jump off his chair, throw his hands up, and scream out his anger. Sarah's words rang in his ears.

Listen. Try to understand.

"That was it. We walked home in silence. That night was the worst night of my life. There he was, sleeping in the bed on the other side of the room, the same bedroom you two slept in, still my brother, but somehow suddenly a totally different person. I stayed awake half the night trying to get over the shock of it all."

Another wave of anger filled Bart.

The worst night of his life....

Bart looked up at the wood studs in the ceiling and took a single deep breath. "So what happened?"

Theodosius looked at the photo of Thaddeus, pressed his lips together, and gently closed the photo album as if he were handling a precious ancient manuscript. "The following week he dropped out of seminary. He continued to attend church to keep up appearances with our parents, but I could see the pain in his face. A few days later he attended his first Exodus meeting. I congratulated him. I told him I was praying for him.

"Over the next month, we hardly spoke. I would ask him how things were going but he didn't say much. One day when we were alone I pressed him for an update. How was he feeling? How were things with Exodus? He said he felt lost, like an orphan. I told him not to give up; God the Father was waiting to welcome him back with open arms.

"Two weeks later he announced to me he had a date with a local girl." Theodosius shook his head. "I'll never forget the look on his face. He may as well have told me he was about to face a firing squad. I wished him luck. He came home after midnight and went straight to bed. I asked him how it went. He said it was awful. The next morning he enrolled at the University of Alabama in the Faculty of Education. He said he wanted to become a teacher. He found a small apartment next to the school. I helped him pack."

Theodosius caressed the cover of the photo album. "Over the next three months we barely spoke. I think I called him twice. Each time he told me the same thing—he was struggling, but he was going to be okay. Each time I told him he just had to keep at it—read scripture, dedicate himself to the Lord, and stick with Exodus. After each call I felt terrible. He didn't sound like he was going to be okay. I promised myself I'd go see him, but I never did. I was too *busy.*"

As if with a great effort, Theodosius pushed himself out of his chair. He turned to the bookshelf and slowly ran his finger over the smooth pine, raising a small plume of dust. He spoke softly, his words barely above a whisper. "We got the call from the police on a Sunday afternoon. He was found by his friend in bed that morning with an empty bottle of scotch, his Bible open to Leviticus, and an empty bottle of sleeping pills."

He returned to his seat, looking to Bart's right with unfocused, wet eyes. "When I got the news, I fell into a state of shock. Later that day, all I could think of was how selfish I'd been. I should have dropped everything and gone to see him. He'd been reaching out for help—I heard it in his voice—and I abandoned him. If I'd been there for him, I know he'd have gotten through this. He'd be alive today." He turned to James. "And then the worst thing of all hit me. He had died without salvation."

A jolt of electricity shot through Bart. "No, Father, no! Please don't think that."

Theodosius turned back to Bart. "For months, I could barely function, but slowly I found a way to live with it, mostly by blocking it out. Of course, the guilt over not reaching out to him never completely went away. Over the years, I couldn't escape painful reminders of it all, some worse than others, but I was always able to deal with them and move on ... until your lecture."

Bart frowned. "My lecture?"

Theodosius retrieved his Bible from a small table to his right. "Homosexuality and the Bible. The instant I heard the words, out of nowhere, like a thunderbolt, Thad came roaring back to me—his tragic death, and my terrible guilt over not doing enough to prevent it. The only thing that got me through it way back then, and even now, is knowing that at least I'd given him the right advice, the only advice I could have given him, in accordance with scripture. And there you were, standing up on that podium, planning to shoot down the one truth that got me through it all. At that moment, already upset over what you'd been saying, I guess I just snapped. I don't remember leaving."

Bart flopped back in his chair, wide-eyed, mouth slightly open, staring at his father. His anger and frustration, so sharp and pure several minutes earlier, now felt strangely wrong. "I had no idea."

"Then came the fire. As we watched James pull Jennifer out of the burning church, not knowing if she would live or die, all I could think of was that I had done this." Theodosius thumped his chest with his fingers. "*I* had burned down the church. I didn't pour the gasoline or strike the match, but I may as well have when I ran out of the church during your lecture and then *conveniently* ignored reports of threats made by Adams."

Bart shot forward in his chair. "Father, that's not even close to fair. I've already told you, if anybody is to be blamed, it should be me. He threatened me straight to my face and, unlike you, I knew she was in there."

"I'll ask you again. If I hadn't fled, would he have burned the church down? We both know the answer, don't we?"

For a brief moment Bart froze. He thrust open his mouth, but at first could elicit little more than an unintelligible grunt. He shook his head as if to jolt his words free. "You can't hold yourself responsible for what other people—"

Theodosius thrust out an open hand toward his son. "But with the grace of God working through James, Jennifer is going to be okay, my anger, depression, and guilt will eventually lessen, and life will go on." He smiled sadly. "At least that's what I thought, until Jennifer told me her secret. Sitting there, looking at her in the bed, I suddenly also saw poor Thaddeus, right next to her. Jennifer Adams and Thaddeus Trask, a generation apart, one dead before the other is born, connected by their secret and my guilt over their terrible suffering. Just like that, my brother's terrible tragedy once again came roaring back to me, larger than life, stronger than ever."

Bart raked his fingers through his hair. "Father, please listen to me. I understand how they're connected, but that doesn't make you responsible for what happened to either of them. Do you hear me?"

"I had no intention of ever telling anyone about Thad.

When you mentioned the word during your lecture, and he sprang into my mind, it was one heck of a shock, but I figured I'd eventually somehow deal with it and move on. I have my church. I'm doing God's work. That's always gotten me through. But this connection between the two of them, bringing me right back to Thad ... this is different. I just can't seem to shake this awful feeling. I know how worried you all are, especially your mother, about me. If I could hide the way I feel, I'd keep it all to myself, but I just can't, not this time. So, here I am, telling you."

Bart tried to process what he'd just heard, but it all just crashed into itself. "You want to know something?" he asked, falling back onto his chair. "I hadn't planned to even mention homosexuality in my lecture. I added it at the last minute for Jennifer."

Theodosius lowered his head. James stared into his hands, his wet eyes blinking rapidly. Junia began to sob. Bart gently touched his father's knee. "Does Mom know about Thad?"

The lines on his face deepened. "She knows he had an overdose."

"Do you plan on telling her the rest?"

"Yes, but not now. I can't tell her now. I could barely tell you."

Bart glanced at his siblings. "Now that we know, we want to help you get through all this. Please tell us how we can help you."

Theodosius grimaced. "I'm sorry for walking out on you. I'm sorry I didn't do the right thing before the fire."

Bart's eyes filled with tears. "Father, it's not your fault, any of it. How can we help you?"

Theodosius looked directly into Bart's eyes. "I don't think you can. I don't think anyone can."

James pulled his chair up to his father and grasped his hand. "Through God's grace *all* things are possible. You know this."

Theodosius slowly rose to his feet, brushed past them, and disappeared down the narrow, steep stairs, leaving Bart, James, and Junia standing in a small circle, staring at each other.

That evening, James and Bart drove in silence to a sports bar outside of town. They selected a booth off in a corner, ordered drinks, and buried their heads in the menu.

James tossed his menu aside. "What are we going to do?"

Bart scanned the burger options. "I don't know. The whole thing is so heartbreaking, especially when he said that he thought poor Thad—" Bart lowered his menu. "Wait a minute. I've got an idea. I wonder...."

"What?"

"Between poor Thad and Jenn, he's got a lot of guilt, right? But I think there's one thing that's hanging over him more than anything else."

"I'm listening."

"What do you think grieves him the most about Thad?"

"That he didn't save his life, obviously."

"Are you sure about that? It may sound crazy, but I don't think so. It's huge, of course, but I don't think it's the biggest thing."

"Really? He sat there and told us—"

"Eternal damnation."

James frowned. "What?"

Bart leaned toward his brother and lowered his voice.

"He's guilty about not saving his brother, for sure, but I think the biggest black cloud hanging over his head is his belief that his poor brother's soul has been lost to the fiery torments of Hell. For Father, a life cut short is one thing, but death without salvation, with nothing but eternal damnation, now that's quite another. I think that weighs on him more than anything."

James returned to the menu. "I think it's a big deal, for sure."

"Well, it just so happens that's the one thing I may be able to help him with."

"How, by trying to convince him there's no Heaven and Hell? Good luck with that."

"No. I'm going to show him the Bible is not anti-gay. Once he realizes that, he'll still have regrets and feel guilty, but he'll feel a lot better about Thad."

James sat up. "Have you lost your mind? You're never going to sell him on that. He knows scripture inside and out. Besides, you heard him loud and clear. That was the reason he left your lecture. That's the last thing he wants to hear."

"I understand, but once he fully realizes the implications of a new interpretation—"

"I'm telling you, you're not going to convince him, not in a million years. It's not about what he wants to believe or not believe, it's about the Word of God, period. Believe me, he knows his Bible. Bible college and Dallas Theological Seminary taught him well."

"Let me ask you. Do *you* think Thaddeus is suffering eternal damnation as we sit here, ordering our food?"

James took a deep breath and looked away.

Bart nodded. "I thought so."

"How dare you claim to know what I think."

"I know what your fundamentalist beliefs tell you to think."

The server returned with a beer and a soda. They ordered burgers and fries. When they were alone, Bart sat back. "So tell me, is Thaddeus burning in Hell?"

James shifted in his seat. "It's not up to me to—"

"Oh come on, don't give me that tired old line. I'm asking you what you think."

"I have faith in the Word of God. That's all I'm going to say."

Bart took a long sip of his beer. "Nice. Have you considered running for political office?"

James sneered. "I think your idea is crazy, okay? If you want to convince him of something, convince him that Thad made his own decisions, from start to finish. It's all about personal responsibility. Believe me, I feel terrible about it, but we need to convince Father he did nothing wrong."

"You really think he's going to buy that?"

"Are you so sure he's not going to buy it, if we both tell him? I say it's worth a try."

Bart shrugged. "Okay, fine, it's worth a try, but I'd first like to try it my way. I believe I can convince him that there's nothing in the Bible telling us that Thaddeus would be punished by God for homosexuality."

"Really? I don't even think there'll be much of a conversation."

Bart smiled. He took another sip of beer. "We may surprise you."

On their way back home from the restaurant, Sarah called Bart.

"Welcome home, sweetheart. How was the flight?"

"Not bad, but I couldn't sleep much. I'm so exhausted I can barely stand. How is Jenn and James?"

"Recovering nicely, I'm pleased to say."

"Excellent. How's your father?"

Bart hesitated. "Still struggling." He considered sharing his bombshell news with her but decided against it. "Get home and crawl into the nest, sweetie. I'll catch up with you tomorrow."

Early the next day, Bart found his father in the garden harvesting asparagus. The sun had just emerged above the trees, casting long shadows over the church and house. Birdsong filled the early morning spring air. Bart looked up into the large oak tree next to the garden. He thought of the big nest in the oak that became home to a family of Northern Cardinals about fifteen years ago. He remembered his entire family gazing at the nest from his bedroom. From that perfect vantage point and with a pair of binoculars they watched in awe as two newborn birdies, their mouths seemingly always open, tweeting baby tweets in harmony, were fed and cared for by the parents.

Bart kneeled next to his father and pulled out several weeds. "You're up early this morning."

Theodosius glanced at his son without breaking his rhythm. "I'm always up at this time."

Bart grabbed a knife from the basket, jumped to another row, and began working. About a half-hour later, with a fresh sheen of sweat on his forehead, dirt under his nails, and a bas-

ket full of asparagus spears, he straightened. "I've been thinking about what you said yesterday." He waited. His father said
nothing. "I was wondering if I could chat with you about what
the Bible has to say about homosexuality."

"I know what it says," Theodosius said flatly.

"I know, but I'd like to … well, just talk to you about it."

Theodosius pushed himself up and took a deep breath.
"Thank you, but that won't be necessary. The written Word
of God is in plain sight for all to see. Dismissing or ignoring
it, no matter how difficult that may be, doesn't change God's
word."

"I'm not dismissing or ignoring the words. I'd simply like
to offer a different interpretation of the words. I'm not saying
the Bible is wrong; I'm saying our standard anti-gay *interpretation* of it is wrong. A lot of Christian scholars happen to
believe that."

"You know, it amazes me that you've actually read the
words and can say this."

"I certainly have read them, in their original languages,
but reading the words, seeing them on the page, isn't enough.
The meaning of these words are not self-evident; they require
interpretation. I'd like to offer you a different interpretation
that says homosexuality is not a sin and, therefore, not punish-
able by eternal damnation. Why? To show you that Thad is
not being punished for this."

Theodosius walked out to the middle of the garden, got
down on his knees, and resumed his work. "I'll say it again.
The Bible is clear on this."

"So, you think I'm wrong. Okay, then *show* me. Show me
why I'm wrong. Believe me, I'm willing to hear your side of

it." Bart knelt next to his father. "You've taught me all my life about how to be a decent man, how to treat others, even how to live the faith, despite having none. Now I'm asking you to teach me again."

Theodosius slowly came to his feet, rubbed his hands on his pants, and wiped his forehead. "Are you going to listen to me?"

"Yes, I promise."

Bart waited. His father said nothing. "Father, it would mean the world to me."

Theodosius looked into his son's eyes. A moment later, he nodded. "Alright, fine."

Bart exhaled. "Thank you. Tell me when. I'll be there."

"Tomorrow night at seven, in the attic. Invite your brother. He'll help straighten you out."

Bart headed back to Junia's place, clenching his fists in triumph. A pang of anxiety suddenly rushed through him. He would only have one shot at this. To have any chance at all, it would have to be his best shot. With only a day and a half to prepare, was he up to the task?

He found Junia and little Thomas awake but still in their beds. "Good morning. Rise and shine, folks! It's a beautiful Spring day."

Following a breakfast of delicious Belgian waffles and a delightful playdate with Thomas, Bart went for a walk and called Sarah.

"Hi honey, are we back to the land of the living?"

Sarah laughed. "We sure are! I can't wait to see you. By

the way, thanks for all the text updates on Jenn while I was away. I'm glad she's doing better."

"I wish I could say the same about my father."

"What's happened?"

"He called Junia, James, and me up into the attic and spilled his guts to us about his brother, our Uncle Thaddeus. I wanted to tell you in person, but I'd rather not wait."

"Tell me everything."

When Bart had finished, Sarah turned on the video call function. Her fingers were buried in her hair, her eyes wide and glistening wet, her mouth open. "I ... I can't believe it."

"I just hope my idea helps him. I don't know what else to do."

"You're doing all you can do, my love, for all the right reasons."

"I'll let you know how it's going at half-time."

"You'd better. Now go get working on this thing."

"Take care, sweet Sarah."

Bart kissed the phone, ended the call, and headed back for Junia's place.

At seven o'clock sharp Bart and James climbed the attic stairs. A driving rain pounded the metal roof just above their heads. Theodosius sat in his chair next to the old wooden bookcase, his palms resting on the black leather cover of his King James Bible in his lap. He glanced at his watch and pointed to the pair of chairs facing him.

Bart sat in the chair to his father's left. He extracted from a satchel his Greek New Testament, his Bibles—New Revised Standard Version and King James Version—and a list of bullet points scribbled in pencil on university letterhead thrown together late the evening before. James, trailing behind his brother, took his seat, crossed his legs, and stared vacantly at the bookcase.

Bart looked into his father's eyes. "Thanks for doing this." Theodosius opened his Bible. Bart glanced at his notes. "All right, so we're here to talk about what the Bible says about homosexuality. You say scripture calls it a sin. I disagree. I'm going to try and change your mind, but who knows, you may change mine. Are we okay with that?"

Theodosius nodded.

"Good. Before we begin I'm going to need to give us a little background about what people two thousand years ago thought about sex in general. It's important because we can't possibly understand what the biblical authors truly meant unless we see things from *their* perspective, based on *their* experience, through the lens of *their* culture two thousand years ago, not from ours."

Theodosius shifted slightly in his seat. To Bart's amazement, James mimicked the exact repositioning.

"As you know, life back then, at the time of Jesus, was strongly male-dominated. The female nature, as men described it, was considered to be inferior, chock-full of less-than-desirable character traits such as physical weakness, deceit, lack of courage, laziness, extravagance, gluttony, and so on. When it came to sex, men called all the shots. The goal of sex was to please the man. Women had no say. Sex was not something you did *with* a woman, it's something you did *to* her. Penetration was all about power and domination by the superior male over the inferior female."

James rubbed the back of his neck as if he'd been sitting for hours.

"Where does homosexuality fit in to these ancient notions? It depends on what exactly we're talking about. Our *modern* understanding of homosexuality doesn't fit in at all. Back then the concept of a homosexual as a person having a biologically determined same-sex attraction, what we would call same-sex *orientation*, didn't exist. The notion of 'a homosexual' would have sounded absurd to them. In fact, the word—"

"Of course it would have sounded absurd," James said, looking at his father.

Bart paused, keeping his eyes on his father. James remained silent. "The word homosexual wasn't even invented until the late nineteenth century. Because of this, it doesn't make any sense to try to talk about what the biblical authors thought of our modern notions of homosexuality any more than what they thought of space travel. Instead, we should be asking what they thought of sexual *acts* involving people of the same gender."

Bart glanced at his notes. "So, what did they think? This may come as a surprise, but we have strong evidence that for the ancients, sexual attraction to either gender was considered completely natural, like eating or sleeping. A person's particular preference was simply considered to be a matter of taste."

Bart paused, inviting a reaction to what he thought must have sounded shocking. His father frowned slightly, but otherwise remained quiet and still.

"So, back at the time of Jesus, under what circumstances were people engaging in same-sex activity? Today, it's usually between two consenting adults. Although it was rarely discussed in the surviving historical record, it seems reasonable to assume that back then consensual same-sex acts were probably known to be taking place just like they are today. Unlike today, however, same-sex activity back then was also occurring under several other circumstances, such as pederasty, which is sex between a socially privileged adult male and an adolescent boy, prostitution, and slave sex."

James turned toward his brother. "Who cares about the circumstances? The act is the same. That's what the Bible is criticizing." He raised his Bible. "As Father says, it's all here, the divinely inspired Word of God, in black and white. The words speak for themselves."

"I've read the words, in English, Greek, Hebrew, and even

Latin. If there's one thing I've learned during my studies, it's this—the words themselves aren't enough."

Theodosius sat up. "The divinely inspired Word of God *is* enough! The Word is everything."

"I don't mean it that way. What I mean is ... it's what I said to you yesterday. The Bible is not self-revealing. Our understanding requires *interpretation* of the text. Over the last two thousand years Christians have done their best to get it right, but on occasion, they've gotten it dead wrong, such as the Bible-based notion that slavery is morally acceptable. The Bible didn't get it wrong; our interpretation was wrong. Same thing here. I think many Christians have misinterpreted what the Bible is saying about same-sex activity. I hope to convince you of that when we get into scripture."

Theodosius shook his head.

Bart opened his King James Bible. "Just so you know upfront, I'm not going to be taking a super deep dive. I just want to touch the surface, to give us something to think about. You know the key passages, the so-called 'clobber passages' that address same-sex activity—Genesis 19, Leviticus 18:22 and 20:13, Romans 1:26-27, 1 Corinthians 6:9, 1 Timothy 1:10, and the creation story in Genesis 1-2."

James rolled his eyes. "I know you can't help yourself but try not to make this sound like one of your lectures at school."

Bart smiled. "I'll do my best." He flipped through his Bible. "So when we look at these passages, we're not going to just look at what the words say. We're going to try to understand what the writers meant by putting ourselves in their shoes, immersed in their culture, not ours. Imagine reading in the Bible 'long distance travel is dangerous and is to be discouraged.' Obviously, you'd know they're not talking about trains, planes, and automobiles. Same thing here."

Theodosius exhaled forcefully. "Naturally."

"Good. So, when we run through the Bible, looking for what it has to say about same-sex activity, one thing should immediately strike us as rather surprising. For an issue that seems to be such an important focus of attention for so many Christians, especially conservative evangelicals, the Bible says virtually nothing about it." Bart waited for pushback, but none came. His father stared at him, impassive.

This isn't like him. What in the world is he thinking?

"Of the roughly thirty-seven thousand verses in the sixty-six books, the Bible devotes less than a dozen verses to this. Jesus doesn't even mention it. You could follow all of Jesus's teachings to the letter and have no idea what he thought about same-sex activity, let alone homosexuality. It's not like he doesn't give us advice about how to live. He implores us numerous times to give away our possessions to the poor, yet for something as important as our sexuality, he says nothing."

James shook his head. "How often does he say 'Thou shalt not kill'? Does that make the commandment any less important?"

"Fair enough, but that's not exactly a controversial issue, now is it? Nobody is wondering where God stands on that one, do we?"

James smirked.

"Alright, so let's start with Genesis 19, the story of Sodom and Gomorrah. We all know the story. Abraham's nephew, Lot, tries to protect two male strangers, angels actually, from gang rape by the angry male mob. He even offers his two virgin daughters as a substitute, but before the gang rape occurs,

God intervenes, saves the angels and Lot, despite offering up his two virgin daughters, and destroys the city.

"So what is the author criticizing here? Well, the Old Testament gives us a strong indication in its thirteen references to the event. Gang rape and inhospitality to strangers are being criticized. Few scholars dispute this. Is same-sex intimacy within a consensual, egalitarian, loving, committed relationship being criticized? No, of course not; that's not what's going on here. Most scholars agree that the story of Sodom and Gomorrah has nothing to say about same-sex intimacy in today's society."

James looked at his father. Theodosius rubbed the cover of his Bible. "I agree, for the most part."

"What don't you agree with?"

"It's a *homosexual* gang rape."

"It's gang rape. Let me ask you—if God, in his infinite wisdom and storytelling virtuosity had intended to criticize consensual, loving, committed, same-sex intimacy that we have today, is this the story he would have inspired?"

"No one on this earth should presume to understand God's ways."

Bart opened his mouth to respond, but closed it. "Let's go to Leviticus." He found the passages in his King James version and read them.

> *You shall not lie with a male as with a woman; it is an abomination.* (Leviticus 18:22)

> *If a man lies with a male as with a woman, both of them have committed an abomination; they shall be put to death; their blood is upon them.* (Leviticus 20:13)

Bart closed his Bible. "I have to say, it seems pretty clear. Same-sex activity between men is being called sinful. There doesn't seem any way around it. This famous word abomination has a clear meaning—a severe moral or ethical transgression. Fair enough, but which other transgresssions did they feel were sufficiently heinous to descend to the level of abomination? Men wearing long hair, for one thing."

Theodosius scoffed. "Sure, except that we both know that words, now and back then, can have different meanings, depending on what you're saying. Poor hygiene and murder are both 'bad,' but I think we'd both agree that only one of these is a grievous sin."

Bart nodded. "Of course, but not likely in this case. Anyway, at the end of the day, should it really matter to us what the Old Testament has to say about how to live our lives in the here and now?"

James's eyes widened. "So now we're questioning the Bible's authority."

"Come on, James. Does anyone really think that Christians should necessarily follow the advice given in the Old Testament? We all know that many of the prohibitions simply don't apply to us, such as crossbreeding animals, sowing two kinds of seed in one field, wearing garments consisting of two different fabrics, rounding off the hair on one's temples, and even getting a tattoo," he said, lifting his arm, exposing a small yin-yang symbol on his outer wrist. "Other teachings seem absurd and are even unethical, such as single women having sex should be stoned; cursing at one's parents warrants death; sex slavery condoned; eternal damnation for lying, levirate marriage, the acceptance of polygamy...."

Why, then, should we necessarily pay any attention to Leviticus regarding this issue if it's clear that we shouldn't see it as authoritative?"

James stood. "So, we can just write off the entire Old Testament?"

"No. I just think we have to see it for what it is, within its historical context."

James shook his head and sat. Theodosius smoothed over a page in his Bible. "What about the Genesis account of creation in Genesis 1 and 2, where God created Adam and Eve—male and female—joined them in marriage, and urged them and their descendants to go forth and multiply? The role of man and woman couldn't be clearer." He snapped his Bible shut. "Man and woman, complementing each other in every way, designed to become one in marriage and grow the human family. He defines a marriage to be between a man and a woman, period. If he had intended, or approved of homosexuality, or same-sex marriage, he would have said so, right there and then. You seem to have forgotten Matthew —

> ... *Have you not read that He who made them at the beginning made them male and female, and said, 'For this reason a man shall leave father and mother, and be joined to his wife, and the two shall become one flesh?'*
> (Matthew 19:4-5)

"I agree, sort of."

Theodosius smirked. "What part of that do you not understand?"

"The writers of these passages are giving humankind

a vitally important directive—go forth and multiply. But why?" Bart pushed himself forward in his chair. "Because their celebration of God's creation hinged on the survival of humankind at a time when life was hard, life expectancies were low, one in three women died during childbirth, and the remaining childbearing woman had to have at least six offspring to maintain the population. Robust procreation was essential to survival. Why in the world would they praise and promote same-sex activity as they understood it? For the times in which they lived, their advice made perfect sense, but it just doesn't make any sense for the here and now, when gay unions are just as loving and committed as with Mom and you, and the planet, if anything, is overpopulated."

Theodosius closed his eyes and threw back his head. "It doesn't change the fact that to survive man and woman must come together to create new life, in accordance with God's grand design. Homosexuals cannot do this."

"I agree, they cannot do this. Does that make them sinners? Where does that leave other people who don't have kids, because maybe they haven't found the right person, can't attract anybody, have fertility problems, would rather not have children, or just wish to be celibate? Are those people sinners? Not according to the Bible. In fact, as you very well know, Father, celibacy is actually encouraged and is even considered to be a gift from God." Bart waved his King James Bible in the air. "In 1 Corinthians 7, Paul encourages celibacy over marriage, counseling people only to marry, if they must, to ethically deal with their uncontrollable sexual desire. As he famously said, 'it is better to marry than to burn with passion.' For Paul, marriage, procreation, and even sexual passion are to be avoided, if at all possible. Is this the advice we should follow, since it comes off the lips of Paul, or does it make more sense to interpret these directives within their appropriate historical context, coming from an apocalypticist who felt the end was near?"

James stretched and headed for the stairs. "I need to take a break."

———❦———

Bart sat in his car and called Sarah.

"How's it going, up in the attic?"

"I don't know. I can't tell."

"Do you think they're listening? You know what they say—when a New Testament historian speaks to a room of Christian fundamentalists, does he make a sound?"

Bart laughed. "Thanks. I needed that."

"Keep at it, sweetheart. All you can do is your best. I wouldn't put much stock on how he's responding to you in real time. He's going to go away and think about what you've said. You've got to give him a chance to process it all."

"I suppose. I should get back. I'll talk to you later."

"What's next?"

"Romans."

"Tough?"

"The toughest."

"But you've got it, right?"

Bart smiled. "I've got it."

"I know you do. I just wanted you to say it."

———√√√——

Bart took his seat next to his brother, opened his Bible to Romans, and began reading.

> *Because of this (idol worship) God gave them over to shameful lusts. Even their women exchanged natural sexual relations for unnatural ones. In the same way the men also abandoned natural relations with women and were inflamed with lust for one another. Men committed shameful acts with other men, and received in themselves the due penalty for their error.* (Romans 1:26-27)

Theodosius looked directly at Bart, straight-faced. "Explain *that* to me."

"On the surface it's a doozy, the New Testament clobber passage that packs the strongest punch, a knockout punch for most conservative evangelicals. But again, what is it really clobbering? This is a powerful example of how historical context is so important.

"As you know, in Romans 1 Paul is bemoaning the idolatrous rejection of God by the Gentiles. In the passage, Paul is clearly condemning same-sex activity, but in what sense? Shameful lusts. Unnatural sexual relations. What does it all mean?"

James smirked. "What does it mean?" He glanced at his father. "It's all right here, in black and white, for all to see. There's no need for interpretation here. Any fool can see exactly what Paul is saying."

Bart took a deep breath. "Oh really? It's that simple, is it?"

"As simple as can be."

"It may seem that way, but if you give me a minute or two, I'd like to offer an interpretation that—"

"Whatever. Go ahead; knock yourself out."

Bart abruptly turned toward his brother. "You know, James, attendance is optional. If you'd rather leave, feel free. I'd be more than happy to continue this with Father, who, as you can see, is allowing me to speak."

For a moment, the two brothers glared at each other. James averted his eyes. "I'm sorry; go ahead."

Bart turned his attention back to his father. "We have Paul's words, but to really understand what he *means* when he speaks of shameful lusts and unnatural sexual relations, we need to dig a little deeper. Since Paul tepidly approved of sexual desire and sexual activity, and only within marriage, if it can't be helped, it shouldn't surprise us that he would find same-sex activity under any circumstance as lustful."

Theodosius leaned forward and nodded his head. "Exactly."

"Fair enough, but what about his 'natural/unnatural' comments? What is he trying to say here?" Bart glanced at his barely legible notes. Unable to find what he was looking for, he dropped the crumpled paper onto his lap. "Okay, so here's the thing. For us, when talking about sex, the word 'natural' brings to mind our complementary physical natures designed for procreation. It's a plumbing thing, right? But is that what Paul was thinking when he used this word?"

James glanced at his father. "What else would he be thinking?"

"That's a great question. What would the words mean to somebody two thousand years ago? Back then, it appears that the words natural and unnatural referred not to our biology, but to the social norms of the day. We know this because of how the word is used in the Bible. For instance, in 1 Corinthians Paul declares that it is unnatural for a male to wear long hair or a woman to expose her hair in public, transgressions hardly rising to the level of sinfulness. Same thing here. When Paul calls same-sex activity unnatural, he's saying it violated a well-established basic social norm of the day about how men should behave sexually."

Theodosius raised his hands. "What if he *is* saying that? I don't see how that changes anything. Just because it's a social norm issue doesn't necessarily make it any less important. Rape happens to be a social norm issue. The fact is, Paul condemned it. That's good enough for me."

"But *why* did he condemn it as socially unacceptable? The why is important if we want to fully understand what Paul was thinking. It makes a difference whether a person thinks murder is unacceptable because it's a heinous violation of human rights or only because he tends to find the sound of gunfire rather unpleasant on a warm summer evening. The why is important."

James rolled his eyes. "The why is obvious."

Bart kept his eyes locked on his father and tightened his jaw. "It's *not* obvious, not from just the passage. In order to understand what Paul meant by the word unnatural we need to step back into his world and remind ourselves of what sex was like back then. As I've said, the arrangement was fiercely patriarchal. Males were—"

James sneered. "So you've said."

Bart turned toward James. "The next time you interrupt me, I'm going to throw you down the stairs. Do you understand?"

James turned away. "Fine, I'll shut up."

"I don't want you to shut up. I just don't want you to cut me off!" He turned back to his father. "Like I was saying, to understand Paul we need to keep in mind that males were socially conditioned to be strong, active, and dominant, not weak, passive, and submissive, like the passive partner in a same-sex union. It's telling that within a male same-sex relationship, usually only the passive, submissive male was ridiculed. Why? Because they were seen as doing the worst possible thing a macho Greco-Roman male could do—take on the unnatural role of the passive, weak, inferior female. The strong active, dominant male, the penetrator, usually wasn't even criticized because he was simply acting in accordance with how a Greco-Roman male should act—powerful and dominant."

Bart smacked the cover of his Bible. "*This* is what Paul, found unnatural—a male forsaking his culturally assigned role of power and domination and adopting a posture of weakness and submission; in a word, acting like a female. For Paul, it's not about the sex act itself or the anatomy; it's the violation of the culturally determined, 'natural' patriarchal social norm in which he lived. To be perfectly blunt, back then it was considered okay for a man to have sex with another man, as long as he was the one doing the—"

"Enough!" Theodosius blurted out.

"Father, these aren't my ideas, or the ideas of some other wacky agnostic liberal. This point of view is supported by solid scholarship."

Theodosius pushed himself up, strolled past the lightbulb toward the stairs and back, looking down, slightly stooped. He sat, opened his Bible, and looked at Bart. "I believe 1 Corinthians and 1 Timothy are the final passages you want to talk about?"

Bart turned to his brother. "James, can I ask you to read these passages?"

James took a deep breath and flipped open his Bible, sending the pages flying, cleared his throat more forcefully than necessary, and began reading.

> *Know ye not that the unrighteous shall not inherit the kingdom of God? Be not deceived: neither fornicators, nor idolaters, nor adulterers, nor effeminate, nor abusers of themselves with mankind, not thieves, nor covetous, nor drunkards, nor revilers, nor extortioners, shall inherit the kingdom of God.* (1 Corinthians 6:9-10)

> *This means understanding that the law is laid down not for the innocent but for the lawless and disobedient, for the Godless and sinful, for the unholy and profane, for those who kill their father and mother, for murderers, fornicators, sodomites, slave traders, liars, perjurers, and whatever else is contrary to the teaching that conforms to the glorious Gospel of the blessed God, which he entrusted to me.* (1 Timothy 1:9-10)

Bart nodded. "So, these clobber passages also seem to pack a pretty powerful anti-same-sex activity punch. In 1 Corinthians, the key words in the King James Version are 'effeminate,' translated from the Greek word 'malakoi,' and 'abusers of themselves with mankind,' translated from the

Greek word 'arsenokoitai'. Over the years, many different translations for these Greek words were given, including the word homosexual, which first appeared in the Bible in 1946. But here's the question—"

James rubbed his neck. "There's always a question with you."

Bart kept his eyes on his father. "There better always be a question, or else we're in deep trouble." He glanced at his notes. "Let's start with the Greek word malakoi. Literally it means soft, as in a soft garment, but it was most often used to refer to weakness of character such as lack of self-control, laziness, cowardice, immorality, deceit, that kind of thing. Since at the time these character traits described the typical female nature, the word was also a derogatory term used to describe women. What do the English translators do centuries later? Do they pick a character trait that best describes the word? Nope. They choose a word for woman—effeminate. The message to men is clear—don't behave in any way, shape, or form like a woman, both in and out of the bedroom."

Bart briefly paused to invite comment. None came. James glanced at their father expectantly. Theodosius held a slight frown, alternating his gaze between Bart and his Bible.

Bart edged forward on his chair. "Now occasionally, the word was used in a clear sexual context—for instance, to describe men head over heels in love who would do anything, including give up their manly dominance, to charm a woman. Back then, that was considered repulsive. As I've said, consensual male same-sex relationships were rarely written about, but when they were discussed, the term was used to describe the passive partner since they were seen to be acting like women, the lowest degradation for a privileged, free Greco-Roman citizen."

Again Bart briefly paused. No comment. Theodosius's frown intensified.

"With all this in mind, what did Paul mean to say when he used the word malakoi? Could he have been criticizing the passive sexual partner in a same-sex relationship, criticizing men who failed to act 'manly' and assume their 'natural' male dominance over women in or outside of the bedroom, or both? We can't be certain, but it seems reasonable to think it was a blanket statement critical of men adopting a female nature."

Theodosius closed his Bible. "When did you read the original manuscripts?"

Bart hesitated. "I didn't say I read the originals; we don't have the originals. But I did read substantial excerpts from most of the New Testament books dating back to the fourth century during my training."

"I see," he said quietly.

The question surprised Bart. He wondered, could it actually be an acknowledgment of scholarship? This would indeed be a welcome first, coming from Pastor Theodosius Trask. On the other hand, as out of the blue as it was, maybe he'd just stop listening.

Keep going. You're almost done.

"Now for the second word, arsenokoitai. Getting to the true meaning of this word is a bigger challenge. Unlike malakoi, the word was rarely used. In fact, Paul is the only biblical author who uses the word. It's occasionally found in lists of vices, which doesn't help with its definition, except to tell us that it must refer to something considered bad. Some scholars think it may be a fusing of two words, arsen, which means man, and koites which means bed, usually with a sexual connotation, suggesting Paul may have used it to describe men who have sex with other men. Although the logic behind this linguistic explanation seems a bit sketchy, we still—"

Theodosius sat up. "Why?"

"Why what?"

"Why is the linguistic thing sketchy? It makes sense to me."

"Oh, because in many cases the fusing of two words doesn't mean anything close to the individual words. Take, for example, the words ... let's see ... understand or chairman."

"Sure, but it does work in some cases, such as mailman."

Bart smiled. "It does indeed. Fortunately, we've got some additional clues to help us. In all the other places the word is found outside of the Bible, it seems to be describing some form of exploitation for gain, possibly economic. But what kind of exploitation? In several instances, the exploitation seems to be tied to something sexual. Because of this, many New Testament scholars feel Paul was likely referring to sexual exploitation. Could he have had prostitution, pederasty, and slave sex in mind? Possibly, but what do the translators do? Instead of—"

James shook his head. "What about Timothy?"

"Same thing. Fornicators and sodomites. From where do these English words originate? When we go back to the original Greek, what do we find? Our old friend, arsenokoitai. What is the writer of Timothy referring to? As in 1 Corinthians, we can't be sure, but he may be bemoaning the exploitation associated with the circumstances under which same-sex activity was sometimes taking place. Now tell me, what does any of that have to do with modern-day homosexuality?"

James glanced at his father. "Brother, to me this sounds like nothing more than just a bunch of speculation."

Bart leaned forward. "Father, I believe that if Paul lived today, when it's not considered shameful within our culture for a male to take on a more submissive role in or out of the bedroom, he wouldn't be calling it unnatural. And if he were to see homosexuality today for what it is, a consensual egalitarian loving relationship which is neither lustful nor exploitive, he wouldn't be calling it sinful. I know this may shock you, but if Paul lived today, I don't think he'd be condemning homosexuality as sinful."

Bart sat back. "It's hard to know exactly what people were thinking two thousand years ago, but if we consider the historical context and add a little common sense, isn't it enough to at least reconsider the traditional hard-core, anti-gay stance? The fact is, many scholars believe that the Bible's anti-same-sex activity stance has nothing to do with modern-day homosexuality."

Theodosius slowly pulled his head up until he found his son's eyes. Bart grabbed his father's forearm. "The divinely inspired Word of God does *not* condemn Thaddeus to eternal damnation. Do you hear me?"

Theodosius looked down at his hands, placed flat on his Bible. He took a deep breath, looked up toward the ceiling for a moment, then back down to his Bible. His eyes glistened. The lines on his face deepened.

Bart slowly stood. "Thanks for listening to me," he said over the crash of torrential rain on the roof. Theodosius remained still, his big wet unfocused eyes staring through his Bible.

Bart turned to James. For a moment they made eye contact. James turned his head away.

Bart collected his things and left the attic.

Bart flopped into his car, sweat on his face, breathing hard. He tried to replay the case he'd made to his father, but all he could see was his father's face, tight with grief. Bart wondered, had he done more harm than good? He rubbed his eyes, shook his head, and drove away.

That evening, after putting little Thomas to bed, filling in Junia, and crawling into bed, Bart called Sarah.

"... You should have seen him when I was finished. He looked terrible."

"It must have been awfully tough on him. I'm amazed he stayed for the whole thing."

"I tried, Sarah, but I think all I've managed to do is to emotionally traumatize him, *again*."

"Bart, the hurt was already there, circulating through him like the blood in his veins. Please give him a chance to consider what you've said. Get a good night's sleep. I'll see you at noon tomorrow."

Bart turned out the light, shut his eyes, and tried to clear his troubled mind.

Bart arrived home the following afternoon. After a buffet lunch at a new Indian place that opened in Chapel Hill and a bike ride with Sarah, he settled in with a cup of coffee to get down to work.

He took his first sip and exhaled. He hadn't realized just how oppressive the events of recent days had been on him. He hoped his impassioned plea to his father would make a difference, but now was the time to let it go, at least for the moment, and get back on track with his life. He had done all he could.

The next several days flew by like the snap of a finger, consumed by schoolwork, reading a number of research papers sent to him for peer review, and working on his new book. Through it all, as always, his father was never far from his mind. Bart thought of calling him, but decided against it. He would call his mother tomorrow after church service to get an update.

Early Sunday morning Sarah and Bart were just about to head out for a bike ride when James called. Bart stiffened. For a moment he stared at the ringing phone. He looked at Sarah and closed his eyes.

"Go ahead, sweetie, answer it."

"Hello?"

"You've got to come back."

"Why? What's wrong? Hang on. Can I put you on speakerphone with Sarah?"

"Yes. It's Father. He just handed the church over to me."

Bart stared at the phone, eyes wide in disbelief. "What? What do you mean handed the church over? What's happened?"

"I don't know. He won't say. After you left, he was quiet but seemed okay. I asked him how he felt. He just shrugged. Yesterday morning, he retreated back to the attic. I let him be, but when he didn't come down for lunch, I went up to check on him. He told me to leave. He spent most of the day and evening up there. He's back up there this morning. Mom can hardly get a word out of him." James exhaled loudly. "Bart, I'm telling you, he looks terrible. I don't think he's eaten since yesterday morning. And just now, when I was up there bringing him some food an hour before church, he handed over the church to me, the whole ... blessed thing! He said he's no longer worthy to lead the people. Can you believe that? Mom is terrified. She wants you here. I know I've been a pain, but ... I want you here too. I need you here."

Bart looked at Sarah. "When?"

"Now. She's worried what he might do."

"What he might do? Did he say anything else?"

"Not really. I tried to tell him Thad made his own choices and all that, but he shut me down. Can you come?"

"I'll call you back in two minutes." He ended the call and closed his eyes.

Sarah raised her eyebrows. "Wow. Coming from your father, that's something. You'd better go."

"Sarah, I'm sorry. I've been so busy these days, and now, just when we have a little time together...."

"Never mind about that." She opened her laptop. "Go pack your carry-on. I'll check on flights."

The initial shock of James's call precluded analysis, but as his head cleared on the way to the airport, Bart began to fear the worst—his attempts to foster a new interpretation of homosexuality in the bible had failed, as he figured it would, cementing his father's notion that he hadn't done enough to save his brother from the torment of eternal damnation. He should have known better than to even try.

He pulled into the Trask driveway five hours later with his guts in a knot, not terribly hopeful that his presence was going to make any difference. He spotted Junia, James, and their mother standing on the veranda. Had they been waiting for him? James opened Bart's car door. "What took you so long?"

"Where is he?"

"In the attic."

"Does he know I'm coming?"

"I just told him."

They found Theodosius in his usual spot, facing the empty chairs, looking at his hands. He caught sight of Bart, locked eyes with him for a moment, then lowered his head, saying nothing.

Bart approached him slowly and sat. He looked at his father's hands—dark wrinkled skin, scattered brown spots, fingers twitching, joined as if in prayer. For a moment, Bart waited, saying nothing. Unable to settle his racing mind, he gently placed a hand on his father's knee. "We're worried about you," he said softly. Several minutes passed, the conspicuous silence filled by the creaking of the wooden floor and the dull roar of trucks and motorcycles in the distance.

Theodosius slowly lifted his head. Bart could see in those big eyes such a deep gloominess as he'd never before witnessed.

"Father, please talk to me. I'm going to sit here as long as it takes to get to the bottom of all this. Talk to me."

After a few moments of silence, James stood. Bart grabbed his arm and yanked him back into his seat.

"James tells me you've handed over the church to him."

Theodosius nodded. "I have."

"Why?"

"It's time James took over," he muttered.

Bart glanced at his brother. "That's funny, he doesn't seem to think so."

Theodosius looked away. "I just think it's time."

"Why? I know it's been awful for you lately with all that's been happening, but that's no reason to walk away from your life."

Theodosius retrieved from the bookshelf a small rectangular photo album with a worn, tan leather cover. From it he extracted two tiny, square, faded black and white photos. He handed a photo to Bart. "The tall thin man in the suit and tie standing next to our tree in the front yard, that's your great-grandfather, Pastor John Trask. What a life. In 1905, at the tender age of thirty, he left his wealthy English parents in Montgomery, built our church, founded and named our town, gave away most of his remaining fortune, and dedicated his life to God." Theodosius handed Bart a second photo. "That's his son, your grandfather, Pastor Ebenezer Trask, as a young boy, standing in front of the very same tree next to his father."

Bart stared at the photos. These Trasks ... they felt so strangely distant in time and essence from himself, yet their flesh begat him, their DNA lived inside him. He touched Ebenezer's face. "I look just like him."

"Of course you do." Theodosius gently took the photos from Bart. "One day, when I was a young teenager, I asked my father, 'what was the most important thing you learned from Grandfather?' He said to be a minister of God is to take on a huge responsibility, not only to preach the Word of God with confidence and conviction, but to be strong enough, both in mind and body, to take on the burdens of the people in the seats, to help and guide them through their troubles, so they can live good lives, within reach of God's grace. He said a preacher without that is nothing but a sad joke, an ineffectual windbag, and a grifter.

"My father took that to heart, carried out that mission, and passed that on to me. I've always prided myself on having that strength, that conviction, that *purpose*. But now, for the first time in my life…."

Theodosius opened his mouth, but no words came. He lowered his head and squeezed his eyes shut. The photo album slid off his lap and hit the floor with a thud, spilling numerous photos onto the wood floor. James flinched. With fear in his eyes, he turned toward his brother. Bart sat quiet and still, stared at his father's hands clutched in prayer, and waited.

Theodosius slowly raised his head. He found Bart's eyes. "How can I stand before my people and lead them with the confidence and conviction of my father and grandfather when I'm no longer sure I have it myself?"

Bart straightened. "What? What do you mean?"

"After you left the other night, I thought long and hard about what you'd said. Then I did some reading, a lot of reading, from numerous sources. The truth is ... I'm no longer sure about it."

Bart's eyes sprang open. He stared dumbfounded at his father. Finally, with great effort, he found his voice. "I'm ... I don't really know what to say. I'm shocked. I didn't expect...."

James frowned. "What do you mean, you're not—"

Theodosius silenced him with an outstretched hand. "How can I preach the divinely inspired Word of God with confidence and conviction to the people when I'm no longer sure of it myself?"

Bart sprang out of his chair. "Father, you haven't lost your confidence and conviction about the Word of God, you're just taking a fresh look at a complex issue. What's wrong with that? If anything, it makes you a better leader, a stronger leader, a leader open to the possibility for change. These things take time, especially something this big. Okay, fine, so you're uncertain. What a massive step forward. Let's keep the discussion going. Keep thinking, reading, studying, reflecting, and yes, praying, until you land on one side or the other. You just need a little more time. I've got a mountain of resources we can look at. We can do this, together."

"It's not just that."

"What do you mean?"

"If I'm right, that it's sinful, it means that after I abandoned him, Thad died without salvation. If you're right, he'd be with God, but it also means I not only abandoned him, I gave him the wrong advice, advice that caused him to ultimately take his own life. I hope and pray for Thad's sake that you are right. But one thing is clear. Either way, I have failed my Lord God. All my life I've tried to do right by Him, but I've failed."

Bart fell back in his chair, limp, blood pounding in his temples, his mouth open, unable to speak.

Theodosius slowly pushed himself up to his feet, brushed past his sons, shuffled across the creaky wooden floor, and quietly descended the attic stairs.

Bart turned to James. "Did you know anything about this?"

"No. He didn't say a word to me."

Bart stared at his father's empty chair. "I sure didn't see this coming."

"Maybe I can talk to him."

"And say what—you gave Thad the right advice; homosexuality is a sin? Is that what you're going to tell him?"

"You think that's what I'm worried about right now, whether it's a sin or not?" James snatched a magazine off the bookshelf, an old National Geographic, rifled through it, and tossed it back. "You know, you really can be cruel sometimes."

"I'm sorry. This whole thing has thrown me into one hell of a tailspin."

"Look, at this point, I don't care what he thinks, as long as he feels better. Poor Thad. We've already had one—" James froze.

Bart grabbed his brother's shoulder and shook him. "Stop it, now, okay? We're going to help him out of this, one way or the other. My bright idea may not have gone as planned, but we'll figure it out together, somehow."

"The problem is Mom and I can't get a word out of him. The only person he seems to want to talk to is you."

"We're just going to have to keep at it."

"Keep at what?"

Bart pulled a photo album off the shelf. "You know, I have this terrible feeling the only person who could get him out of this is not here to help him."

James ran his fingers over the top of the dusty bookcase. "Where do we go from here?"

"No idea." Bart clenched his jaw. "Don't worry; we'll come up with something."

Bart's eyes fell on a tattered old black and white photo of his maternal grandmother resting in a crooked rusty silver frame on the top shelf. He flashed back to his childhood, when she would secretly give him cookies before dinner, as long as he promised not to tell. He picked up the frame and smiled sadly. "James, do you mind if I just sit here a while? I'd like to … I don't know, just sit here."

"I'll go see Mom."

Bart placed his father's chair a little closer to the large bookcase, within reach of the numerous old leather-bound albums containing photos of his parents and their families. He'd known they were here since his childhood, but other than an occasional disinterested glance over his mother's shoulder years ago, he'd ignored them.

He reached for the album his father had been perusing and scanned it for photos of his Uncle Thad. He suddenly wanted to know more about him. A couple of photos couldn't possibly tell him very much, but it was all he had.

Racing through four albums, he found lots of photos,

mostly faded color images, from infancy up until high school graduation. Many of the photos were of Thad and big brother Theodosius, seen in all types of settings—birthdays, holidays, sporting events, at school, and in church. In many of the photos, the boys were smiling or laughing, mostly at each other. One photo, a birthday celebration at the family kitchen table, the same table at which Bart celebrated his first eighteen birthdays, took his breath away. He retrieved it from its plastic covering to take a better look.

A young Theodosius—the back of the photo indicated he was ten years old—sat behind a huge round white cake with multicolored candles, smiling broadly, posing for the camera. A slightly shorter Thaddeus sat at his big brother's left side, his arm awkwardly draped over the birthday boy's shoulder, looking at him with a silly loving grin. Bart smiled. Such love between brothers, such unmitigated childhood joy, all from a small, faded photo buried in the far corner of a musty attic. The photo suddenly became blurry. He wiped his eyes, took a picture of it with his phone, and carefully replaced it in the album.

After several minutes of just staring into empty space, Bart revisited some of the other photos. He looked into his uncle's eyes, trying to construct a portrait of the child, the boy, the young man, wishing he could have met him, talked to him, become friends with him, and ultimately supported him through his terrible struggle.

He spotted the corner of an additional album he had missed, separated from the others, partly buried by a stack of ancient National Geographics and other magazines. A cloud of dust arose, triggering several sneezes as he extracted it from its hiding spot. He found a few additional photos from Thad's high school years and college, including one of him driving. This photo seemed to be raised slightly in its plastic covering. Bart spotted a tattered edge of faded white paper behind it.

Bart removed the photo and found the left upper front part of an envelope addressed to Thad. He replaced it under the photo and was about to close the album when he froze. He took another look at the envelope. The address … it was a P.O. box. His eyes shot up to the left upper corner.

Anthony McInnis Perry
63 Bramblewood Court
Birmingham, AL

Why the P.O. box? He carefully examined the album for a letter, or any other similar items, but found nothing. He was about to replace the envelope fragment behind the photo when he caught his breath.

Could he be Thad's partner?

Could he still be alive? He'd be about sixty. Bart slipped the envelope fragment into his pocket and pulled out his phone.

Let's see. The name is unique enough.…

After almost an hour of perusing social media and Google, he found numerous people called Anthony Perry, but no Anthony M. Perry, and none that seemed to fit the age range. A number of profiles had no photo, and all were private. Could one of these be him?

After another few minutes of checking on a few other sites, Bart gave up. He replaced the fragment behind the photo, replaced all the photo albums, and headed toward the stairs.

Three steps down he abruptly stopped, sat on the steps, and once again pulled out his phone. Ten minutes later, he gasped.

Anthony McInnis, Birmingham, Alabama

He stared at the photo of a well-groomed man of about sixty with a round face, bald head, and close-cropped gray beard. Could this be him? Bart pulled up a lookup service. A few minutes later, he had an address and phone number. He went back into the attic, sat in his father's chair, and stared at his phone.

Why are you doing this?

He entered the phone number and stared at it, his finger hovering over the call icon. A moment later he took a deep breath and touched the screen.

On the fourth ring, a man answered. "Hello?"

"Hello. Can I speak to Anthony McInnis please?"

"This is he. How can I help you?"

A surge of electricity coursed through Bart. He hesitated. "This is Bart Trask, Thaddeus Trask's nephew. Were you a friend of Thad's?"

Bart waited. The man said nothing.

"I never met my uncle. I thought I'd—"

"How'd you get this number?" the man asked harshly.

"I found your name on an envelope tucked behind a photo of him in my father's attic. I was hoping—"

The connection dropped. Bart sat up, thunderstruck.

I've found him.

What to do now?

Several minutes later he made his decision.

He turned out the light and headed downstairs.

The following evening, soaked from a torrential downpour, heart pounding, and wondering if he were doing the right thing, Bart rang the bell of the large two-story red brick home. After a second ring the door flew open. A tall, thin, clean-shaven man of about sixty with kind, tired eyes, stooped shoulders, and short white hair stood before him. "Can I help you?"

Bart hesitated. "Ah ... my name is Bart Trask. I'm looking for Anthony McInnis."

The man frowned. "What's your business with Mr. McInnis?"

His stomach tightened. "I'd like to talk to him about an old friend of his, my uncle Thaddeus Trask."

The man he had seen in the Facebook profile suddenly appeared. "What the hell are you doing here? How did you get my address?"

"I'm so sorry to intrude like this, but I felt I just had to speak to you."

"Well, you can turn around and get out of here."

"Please, listen to me. I just found out about poor Thad— his coming out, his struggle, everything. When I heard about it, it broke my heart. It made me sick. I desperately need to talk to you."

"Who told you about him?"

"My father."

Anthony's eyes narrowed. "Did he send you here?"

"No. He doesn't know about you." Bart waited, soaked to the skin, his pleading eyes locked onto Anthony. "Can I please talk to you?"

Anthony's face softened. He stepped back. "Come in." He led Bart into the family room. "Wait here, I'll get you a towel."

Several music stands, an amplifier, stacks of sheet music, and three flutes sitting upright in their stands caught his eye. Anthony returned with two towels, placing one on a straight-backed wooden chair and handing the other to Bart.

"Thank you so much. You play?"

"Yes." He motioned Bart to the chair. "Have a seat. Can I get you some water?"

"That would be fine, thanks."

A moment later, Anthony placed a bottle of water on the oval-shaped glass coffee table next to Bart.

"This is Patrick, my brother."

Bart pushed out a smile. "Pleased to meet you." He took a sip of water and turned to Anthony. "Can I ask you how you were connected to Thad?"

Anthony flopped onto the couch opposite Bart's chair. For a moment he stared at Bart blankly. "We were friends," he said dispassionately.

"I'm sorry, but I have to ask. Was he your partner?"

Anthony closed his eyes. He nodded. "Yes, he was my partner."

"I figured. I just needed to make sure. I'm so glad I found you."

Anthony rested a foot on the edge of the table. "I'm sorry about my initial reaction. Before this goes any further, I need to tell you something." His eyes narrowed. "I hate your father's guts for what he did to Thad."

Bart straightened. "Could you please tell me about my uncle? I know so little about him."

Anthony's face softened. "He was a good man. He was kind and generous. He loved people. He had a great sense of humor, despite what he was going through."

"I can only imagine. If you don't mind me asking, what was it like for him? I know it must have been terrible. I just need to know."

Anthony placed his hands behind his head and looked up. "He had a ... how can I say it ... a silent suffering about him. I could see it in his eyes. I tried to help him. 'Who cares what people think?' I would say. I think there were times when I was getting somewhere, but then, just when I thought I was making progress, he would bring up the Bible and fall back into a state of uncertainty."

"What did you tell him?"

Anthony shrugged. "It's a great book, but at the end of the day it's just a book written by a bunch of real people a long time ago when life was a lot different. He listened, but it only served to increase his confusion and despair. On the one hand he would say the Bible was the Word of God, and the Bible said certain things about homosexuality, whether we liked it or not. On the other hand he had such a hard time understanding and accepting why God would punish him for being who he was."

"Was he in seminary then?"

"Yes."

Bart wiped his face and neck with the towel. "That must have been terribly frustrating for you. Why did you stay with him?"

"It wasn't easy, but he was such a sweet man. I loved him. I don't know, maybe I thought I could fix him, or something. Every once in a while, I actually thought I saw real glimmers of hope, but all that went right down the drain right after he spoke to your father."

"What happened?"

"He left seminary, joined Exodus, the gay conversion therapy organization, and broke off our relationship, that's what happened."

"I see."

"When he told me we had to split, we were both crushed. He begged for my forgiveness and understanding. He said he would need that to make it through."

"Did you give it to him?"

Anthony shook his head. "Not right away. I was just so frustrated with him and furious with your father, I couldn't see straight. I begged him to reconsider. I threw everything I had at him to change his mind, but I just couldn't do it. Finally, after a couple of days, I told him I understood and accepted it. It was a lie."

Bart took a long sip of water. "And forgiveness?"

"There was nothing to forgive."

"That couldn't have been easy."

"No, but I loved him, so I let him go. I told him it was a terrible mistake, that he was trying to destroy his authentic self, but I wished him well. I told him if he ever wanted to talk, I'd be there for him."

"Did you see or talk to him again?"

Anthony rose and walked over to the window and stared outside. "I saw him once, in the grocery store, about a month after we split up. He said he was doing well, but he sure didn't look it. He'd lost a lot of weight and looked exhausted. I wanted to say something, do something, but what could I say or do? That was it. I left my groceries in the cart in the middle of the aisle, ran out of the store, sat in my car, and pounded the steering wheel, thinking of how much I still missed him and hated your father."

"What happened after that?"

"He killed himself two months later," he said, staring out the window.

"I heard." Bart paused. "How did you find out, I mean, when he died?"

"His neighbor called me when he didn't answer his phone or door."

"Who found him?"

"I still had a key to the apartment. I think I'd forgotten to give it to him when I left, or maybe I'd hoped we'd get together again. I don't know. Anyway, I opened the door. I found him in the bed with his open Bible, an empty bottle of scotch, and some empty pill bottles in the bed. I touched his arm. He was stone cold."

Bart sat straight and still as a post. Anthony returned to the couch.

"When I saw him I staggered out into the hall and slumped to the floor. I just wailed, loud enough to wake the dead. People came out into the hallway. I'm not really sure what happened after that. I only know that my grief quickly became anger, an anger I never thought possible. At that moment, I wanted to kill your father. I wanted to go over to his house and choke him to death with my bare hands. I actually thought about it for a second."

"I'm so sorry, Anthony. I didn't mean to crack all this wide open."

"It's okay. It never really goes away anyway. Why did he tell you, after all these years?"

Bart took a deep breath. "That's one of the reasons I'm here. Something terrible has happened. What I'm going to tell you.... I just want to prepare you, warn you really, a lot of it involves my father. I know how you feel about him, Anthony. I understand, completely. Please know that I'm not here to defend him. You'll see that as I tell my story, but I just wanted to say that upfront."

Anthony nodded. "Go ahead."

Bart suddenly realized Anthony knew virtually nothing about him. How does one summarize the life of a secular humanist borne out of a family of Christian fundamentalists in a word or two?

Just tell your story.

After giving a mini-biography of himself, Bart briefly reviewed the events that led to his father's existential crisis. Anthony listened quietly, barely moving on the couch, expressionless.

"Anthony, I know how you feel about him. To be honest, I believe he did give Thad bad advice and should've been more supportive, but he doesn't deserve to be buried alive for it. Unless he can somehow find a way to deal with his guilt, I don't think he's going to make it. I think it's going to kill him.

Despite all he did, and didn't do, he doesn't deserve that. I've tried to help him, but it looks like I may have made a mess of it. I just don't know what else to do."

"So, you've come here to tell me. Why?"

"I guess I was hoping that you'd be willing to try to convince him that although he may have made some mistakes, it ultimately wasn't his fault that Thad died."

Anthony locked onto Bart's eyes. "I can't do that," he said quietly.

"Can I ask you why?"

"Because it *was* his fault."

Bart pushed himself toward the edge of his chair and leaned forward. "Anthony, he feels terrible about what he did. He's trying to do right. He's even seriously reconsidering how he feels about homosexuality. For us that may not seem like much more than simply seeing the truth, but for him, in his world, for the people who look up to him, it's massive."

"That may be so, but it doesn't change what he did. Your father pushed Thad in the wrong direction and without so much as lifting a finger watched him spiral down out of control until he took his own life. Your father has Thad's blood on his pious hands. I know it, with all my heart and soul. I can never forgive him for that."

Bart tossed the wet towel onto the table, knocking over the empty plastic water bottle. "So, that's it? You won't try to help him?"

Anthony stood. His eyes narrowed. His neck tightened. His words, previously unthreatening, were now suddenly sharp, their distinctness exaggerated, their volume increased. "I'll say it again. When Thad needed him most, when he was struggling and suffering, your father did absolutely nothing to help him. Nothing is going to change that."

"Yeah ... kind of like when you saw him in the grocery store, huh?"

Anthony's eyes flew open. For a moment he hesitated. "That wasn't the same at all."

"You're right, that wasn't the same at all. What was I thinking?"

Anthony stepped around the coffee table toward Bart until their feet almost touched. "I'd like you to leave now. I don't want to ever see or hear from you again. Do you understand? I'm only going to say this once."

Bart stood his ground. "Thanks for the water. I'll see myself out." He threw open the front door and stepped into a driving rain, feeling sick with helplessness and anger, wishing he'd never come.

Bart threw himself back into his work, devoting most of the following week to university-related matters. Nightly calls to James hadn't been encouraging. Their father had continued to shuffle around the house, saying little, eating poorly, and staying up half the night sitting alone on the front veranda. James had encouraged him to take back the church but to no avail.

Bart rose with the sun on Saturday morning already exhausted from yet another night of fitful sleep. Echoes of his disastrous meeting with Anthony continued to reverberate through him, further crippling his attempts at constructive thought. Sarah had ambitious plans for them—brunch at their favorite restaurant, an afternoon hike in the woods, and a fancy evening out to dinner. He would do his best to enjoy the day, but his heart wasn't in it. He would have rather found a quiet place, turned out the light, closed his eyes, cleared his troubled mind, and figured out something, anything, to ease his father's misery.

While Sarah slept, Bart poured a cup of coffee, half-heartedly opened his laptop, and stared at his background image, a magnificent photo of Mother Earth taken from space, a splendid tapestry of deep blues and white swirls. Was there something, anything out there, to help his father, even only a little? It sure didn't feel like it. After about fifteen minutes of disorganized thought-fragments he wondered if there might be someone at UNC who could help him with this. Nobody came to mind. He did some sniffing around in the staff directory. Nothing. Who would he be looking for anyway?

He shuffled into the shower. The hot water felt good but didn't bring any answers. He stepped out, wondering if he had even washed his hair. He reached for the towel and froze.

Wasn't there an organization....

Dripping wet he rushed to his laptop. Twenty minutes later he pounded the table. He had found his man—Pastor Jeremy Vines, a devout Christian and founder of the Reformation Project, an organization dedicated to the inclusion of the LGBTQ community in the Christian church. With nothing but a towel draped over his shoulders Bart threw down an email to the pastor briefly outlining the issues at hand and asking for a conversation.

Sarah stood before him, frowning. "What in the world are you doing? There's a puddle of water all the way from the shower. I have to say, though, I don't mind the look."

Bart snapped his laptop shut. "I'll tell you on the way to brunch. I'm suddenly starving."

Four hours later, while getting ready for their hike, his phone rang. He snatched it off the kitchen table, almost dropping it. The unfamiliar number quickened his pulse.

"Hello?"

"Hello, is this Bart? It's Jeremy Vines."

Bart nodded excitedly to Sarah. "Pastor Vines! Thank you so much for calling."

"You're quite welcome. Is now a good time to talk?"

"Absolutely."

"Great! Please tell me more about your father and uncle."

They talked for an hour and a half. The pastor asked a few questions but otherwise said little.

"Jeremy, I just think that if you can somehow convince him that God doesn't condemn people for their sexual orientation he'll stop torturing himself over the uncertainty of it all and take comfort knowing that Thad isn't being eternally punished. Whatever you could do for his guilt for how he feels he treated Thad would also be immensely appreciated."

"Leave it to me. I've got a few ideas up my sleeve that may prove to be quite helpful. No guarantees, of course, far from it, but I'm thinking I may be able to help him, on both fronts."

"That would be quite wonderful. Of course I'll pay for your time, your expenses, everything."

"That won't be necessary. The foundation has a fund for this kind of thing."

"Thank you! When can you come?"

"How about next weekend? I could fly into Birmingham Friday evening, see him anytime on Saturday, and catch a return flight Sunday morning."

"Perfect. Let's make it two. I'll let you know if the time needs to change." Bart paused. "What should I say to him?"

"Tell him a friend of yours, a devout Christian, has agreed to come in and speak to him. Please email your father's address to me. I'll take care of the rest."

"Thank you so much, Jeremy. Believe me, this means more than I can say."

"I can tell. I promise I'll do my best. That's all I can give you. I'll send you my itinerary when confirmed."

"I'll see you then."

Bart ended the call and called his father. Theodosius answered in a raspy flat tone.

"Hello."

"Father, it's Bart. Are you okay? You sound—"

"I'm okay," Theodosius said quietly.

"I'm going to get right to the point. I have a request. A friend of mine, a very devout Christian minister, would like to talk to you about the struggles you're having."

Bart waited. No response. "Father, can you hear—"

"You've been talking to people about this?"

"Just him. You can trust him with your life. He understands all this. He'd like to visit next Saturday."

Bart again waited. Once again, his father said nothing. "Please, Father. He's a good man and a strong Christian. Will you see him? Please?"

"I don't see the point."

"Will you give him a chance?"

"Who is he?"

"His name is Pastor Jeremy Vines. He's from Wichita, Kansas. He'll be in Birmingham next weekend. He can stop by next Saturday afternoon at two, or any other time you'd like. Will you see him?"

Bart waited. Theodosius said nothing. Bart began to pace. "Father, will you see him? Please?"

"You say he's a devout Christian?"

"Yes, *absolutely*," Bart nearly shouted, filling his voice with all the reassurance he could muster. "I *promise* you, he's—"

"Okay, fine, I'll see him."

Bart shut his eyes and exhaled. "Thank you. Is two o'clock okay?"

"I suppose. Will you be there?"

"Yes, if that's okay, but just to listen and learn. I won't say a word."

"You know, son, you can't change the past with the future."

"I'll see you then." Bart tossed the phone onto the bed and celebrated with a fist pump.

Sarah emerged from the bedroom. "How'd it go?"

"We're all set for next Saturday afternoon," he said, beaming.

"He's coming?"

"He sure is!"

"You think he can help?"

Bart shut his eyes and began to sway, his only dance step. "He seems to think so. We can hope."

"And pray."

Bart smiled. "Yes, and pray."

33

The following Wednesday afternoon Bart arrived at Junia's place. After a barbeque and an exciting game of hide and seek, Bart collapsed onto a chair on the back deck with a lemonade, remembering the great hide and seek games of his youth. The crickets sang out in unison, sharp and clear under the star-filled night sky. Through the open window he could hear the splish-splash of a certain precious little boy suffering through his nightly bath. He turned toward the window and smiled.

Alone, with only the night sky and cricket-song, his thoughts turned to Jennifer. He had promised to update her on any significant developments. Those he had, in abundance. He pulled out his phone.

"Hey Jenn, it's Bart."

"Hey. Long time no speak. How are you?"

"I'm okay. How are you feeling?"

"I'm doing good. My breathing is pretty well back to normal, except for a dry cough I can't seem to shake. The burns are healing well."

"Great. I'll let James know." Bart glanced at his watch. "Listen, I'm here, at Junia's place. I was wondering, would you like to meet somewhere, maybe for a coffee or drink? I'd like to bring you up to date on my father."

"Yes, of course. Why don't you just come over to my place?"

"I'm on my way."

Jennifer greeted him with a smile and welcomed him inside. Bart was struck by the extensive scarring scattered over her arms, neck, and face. He sat on the edge of a tattered leather recliner. Jennifer sat opposite him on the matching tattered, slightly lopsided couch. The small, narrow family room was dark and cluttered and held a faint odor of dirty socks. Bart caught himself looking around, then pulled his eyes back to her.

She blushed. "I'm so sorry. I haven't had the chance to get rid of all this junk. As you can see, my father lived like a pig. My bedroom is really much cleaner. Let's sit on the porch. Can I get you a beer?"

"Sure."

Jennifer returned with two beers. They clinked bottles. Bart took a sip. "How's Tracy doing?"

Jennifer smiled. "Great. She'll be stateside in seventeen days."

"Fantastic! What then?"

"Then we get the hell out of here."

"Where to?"

"Who knows. Who cares? Anywhere but here."

"Please let me know so I can invite myself to see you guys."

She laughed. "You won't have to invite yourself. How's Sarah?"

"She's doing well. She had a great trip to Israel. She sends her love."

"When am I going to see her?"

"She promises to get down here as soon as she can. Unfortunately, she's crazy busy coming to the home stretch of her studies, but as soon as she's done, she'll be here, or wherever you guys happen to be."

"I can't wait."

Bart forced a brief smile. He took a long sip of beer. "I'd like to tell you about what's been going on since you saw my father."

"How is he?"

"I'm afraid to say the news isn't all that good."

"I'm sorry to hear that. Tell me."

Bart sat back and brought her up to date. She listened intently, sipping her beer, interrupting him only occasionally for clarification. When he finished he retrieved the photo of Thad and Theodosius from his phone and showed it to her. "The two brothers at my father's birthday party. Isn't that a great pic?"

"Thad looked like a happy kid," she said with a bittersweet smile.

"Yeah."

"Your uncle would be proud of you, Bart."

"I don't know, Jenn. I'm trying, but…."

"Hey, the pastor may make a huge difference."

Bart shrugged. "Maybe. I don't know. When I discovered him I was pretty excited, but now, I'm not so sure. I guess I just don't want to get my hopes up too high."

"I'm amazed you found McInnis."

"Yeah, well, part of me wishes I'd never seen that envelope."

"You can't mean that."

Bart caught sight of a crucifix hanging on the wall behind Jennifer. "All I did was rip open a bad memory for the poor guy and remind him how much he hates my father."

"Are you going to go back and see him?"

"Why in the world would I do that?"

"To try again."

Bart shook his head. "Not a chance. I looked into his eyes, and I didn't like what I saw. I'm worried he might beat me up, or worse."

Jennifer paused. "Well let's hope Vines can spin his magic and turn things around."

Bart finished his beer, stood, and gave her a hug. "I'll let you know how Saturday goes."

Bart arrived at his parent's house on Saturday afternoon at one-thirty, a half-hour prior to the expected arrival of Pastor Vines. His mother stared out the window from her favorite rocking chair in the living room.

"Where's Father?"

"In the garden."

"Has he forgotten about the pastor's visit?"

She stopped rocking. "Your father spoke to me this morning," she said quietly.

Bart slowly approached her. "What do you mean, spoke to you?"

"In bed, before we got up, he told me everything." She pressed her lips together. "You should have seen him, lying flat on his back, looking up at the ceiling. His face was white as the sheet covering him. His eyes ... they were lifeless, as if he'd just been condemned for life. I tried to hug him. He pushed me away. I told him that he'd done nothing wrong, that the fire wasn't his fault, that poor Thad was resting in blessed peace, but I don't think he even heard me. I haven't seen him since."

Bart hugged her, nearly tipping them both over backward. "Don't worry, it's going to be okay. Do you hear me? The pastor is going to help."

With a surprisingly strong arm, Linda pushed her son aside and sprang out of the rocker. "What if he doesn't? What then?" She grabbed her son's shoulders and shook him. "Bart, his life is in your hands!"

Bart wrapped his arms around her. "He's going to be okay, I promise."

Linda broke the embrace. "Then go out there and drag him back in here."

"Are you going to stay, for the pastor?"

She hesitated. "No, I'm too upset. I'll be in my room. I can hear everything from there."

Bart found his father on his knees at the edge of the garden. His hands were covered in dirt. His face glistened with sweat.

"Have you forgotten about Pastor Vines? He's due to arrive in half an hour."

Theodosius extracted a clump of weeds, knocked off the excess dirt, and tossed them into the half-filled basket. He slowly came to his feet, slapped the dirt off his knees, and wiped his forehead with the back of his sweaty hand. "I'll be done in a minute."

Bart entered the family room, wondering just how big a catastrophe this was going to be. Several minutes later Theodosius entered the house and headed upstairs. The shower came on. He reappeared fifteen minutes later in a clean set of clothes and sat in his recliner.

Shortly after two, a knock came at the screen door. Bart jumped up and opened it. Before him stood a tall, well-built, clean-shaven man in his fifties. He wore light gray slacks, a white dress shirt, and a black sports jacket.

"Pastor Vines?"

"Yes indeed. You must be Bart Trask."

"I am. Come in." Bart escorted him into the family room. "Pastor Jeremy Vines, I'd like you to meet my father, Pastor Theodosius Trask."

The two men shook hands. Vines smiled warmly. "Pastor Trask, I'm very pleased to meet you." Theodosius nodded and offered a weak smile.

Vines sat on the couch facing Theodosius. A wooden coffee table separated them. Bart served the two men iced tea and sat on the other end of the couch.

"Thanks for agreeing to see me. I don't know how much Bart has told you about me, so I thought I'd give you a thumbnail sketch. I'm a Christian minister of a large non-denominational church in Wichita, Kansas. I consider myself a devout Christian who believes, with all his heart and soul and strength, that the Bible is the divinely inspired Word of God and that salvation comes to all through the belief in the death and resurrection of our Lord Jesus Christ."

Bart glanced at his father. The tightness in his face seemed to lessen.

"Out of his concern for you, your son called me last week to ask me for some advice and, if possible, to help you with your struggles."

"Why you?"

"That's a good question. Out of many, he picked me because of my particular interest in homosexuality."

Theodosius's eyes narrowed. "Particular interest?"

Vines smiled kindly. "I'm not homosexual. I've been married for twenty-six years and have three grown children."

Theodosius glanced at Bart. "But you have a particular interest."

"Indeed I do. I've been a minister for twenty years. For the first fifteen years, in accordance with the traditional view of the Bible, I took a hard stand against homosexuality. I considered it a sin and worthy of exclusion from the church. I rarely spoke about it directly, but my congregation knew where I stood. That all changed five years ago when I gave a sermon on the warnings Paul has given us about the various sinful acts that will exclude us from the gates of Heaven, including homosexuality."

Bart glanced at his father. Theodosius sat bolt upright in an armchair better suited to a more relaxed posture. His eyes, if not inviting, gave no indication of contempt.

"The sermon seemed to be well received. I'd forgotten about it until I started getting mail from people protesting my anti-gay stance, complaining it was excluding many committed Christians from the faith. Of course, I paid little attention to these. All that changed one fine Saturday morning when I came upon a group of seven people sitting in a circle in front of the main entrance of the church. Their heads were bowed, as if in prayer. A middle-aged woman with tears in her eyes stepped forward. She told me they were gay members of the church praying for God to change my heart on homosexuality."

Vines crossed his legs and draped his arm across the top of the couch. "I gave them the party-line response—the Bible is the Word of God—and implored them to get right with God. I began to walk away. The woman asked me, 'then what are we to do?' I kept walking. I was stopped in my tracks by the voice of a young man telling me I had it all wrong, that the Bible was not anti-gay. He pulled out three books from a satchel and thrust them toward me, pleading with me to read them. I shook my head and walked away. I entered my church, fuming. A moment later the church door opened. The books hit the marble floor with a loud thud. The door slammed shut. I hovered over them as if they were a family of rattlers ready to spring up and bite me. Finally, I picked them up, sat in the back row, and took a look. To shoot down their nonsense, I had to know what they were saying."

Vines paused, as if inviting a response. Theodosius sat motionless, stone-faced.

"What I read, together with other materials, all from committed Christians, shocked me. I tried to dismiss it all, but I couldn't. Within three months, I had managed to read virtually everything available on the topic, from all sides. At the end, I was convinced. That young man who had the audacity to challenge me that morning on the church steps ... he was right, for all the reasons your son has already given you. The Bible is not anti-gay."

Vines jumped up and walked behind the couch. His hands suddenly joined the conversation. "You should have seen me. I went into such a depression, I could barely function. I lost twenty-five pounds. I couldn't sleep. I could barely eat. I even left my church. I prayed for forgiveness for all the lives I'd hurt until I was blue in the face, but it didn't seem to matter. Then, one day, all at once, through the grace of God, it came to me. Instead of regretting the past, I needed to start being part of the solution. But what solution?

"That's when I created the Reformation project, a multidisciplinary coalition of Christians, both gay and straight, whose mission it is to advocate for inclusion of the LGBTQ community into Christianity through education and support. I started this a little over four years ago. Now we have a worldwide organization of about three thousand active members committed to changing hearts and minds within the Christian world."

Theodosius cleared his throat with a weak cough. "Not within the evangelical world."

"True enough, but remember how long Christians believed the Bible supported the notion that the earth sat at the center of the heavens? To be blunt, and with all due respect, benign ignorance is a stubborn stain to cleanse. Change may be slow to come within the evangelical community, but many denominations within our vast Christian community have now adopted some degree of inclusion. I'll send you a recent report on where the various denominations stand. Slowly but surely things are changing. You can change too. It's not easy, but you *can* change."

Theodosius stared at the coffee table between them.

Vines returned to the couch. "Pastor Trask, do you think it's possible for Christians to misinterpret important teachings of the Bible?"

"Yes, of course."

"Based on everything you've heard and read and studied, do you think it's possible for Christians to have misinterpreted the Bible's view on homosexuality?"

Theodosius closed his eyes and tilted his head back. "I don't know. I just don't know."

Vines nodded. "You're uncertain. That's okay. In fact, it's

much better than okay. It takes a lot of courage to step away from your comfort zone. I admire you for that. Can I ask you why you feel uncertain?"

Theodosius shook his head. "I just ... I'm just not sure about it."

"I believe I know why you're having such a hard time with this. I believe I know why, because I lived it myself. It's not about the strength of the case for or against inclusion found in the Bible outlined by your son. It's about what you've always *believed*, not just in your head, but in your heart. It's just so hard to even consider the possibility that you may have been incorrect about something you were so sure about your entire life. Am I right?"

Theodosius pushed himself up and shuffled over to the screen door. He slowly ran his fingers over the fine mesh, then let his arm fall limp at his side.

Vines stood and turned toward him. "Believe me, it was the toughest thing I ever went through, but if *I* could do it—"

Theodosius slammed the screen door frame with his hand. "For Thad's sake I *want* you to be right, even if it means I had it wrong, even if it means I did the worst of all things, gave him the wrong advice that ultimately led to his death. For Thad's sake I would gladly take that disgrace, I would gladly accept God's judgment for these terrible things."

Vines shook his head. "No, Theodosius. There would be no punishment from God for what you did, or failed to do. In God's eyes, it's not what you do, it's why you do it. With a heart full of love and the best intentions you followed traditional Christian doctrine, the only thing you knew. I'm suddenly reminded of somebody else who got it wrong. As an orthodox Jew he persecuted Christians before converting to Christianity to become its greatest champion. Maybe you've heard of him. His name is Paul. I'm sure he also felt terrible guilt and regret, but I think you'll agree he was able to reconcile with God and move forward in a magnificent way."

Theodosius nodded. "Paul did inflict pain and suffering, no doubt, but I wonder, did he know what it felt like to inflict it upon his own flesh and blood, and then ignore the suffering until the misery is so great that...? Did he know that terrible feeling? Does forgiveness, even God's forgiveness, wash *that* feeling away?"

Vines hesitated. He thrust himself forward to the edge of the couch. "Theodosius, we must trust in the power of His grace as long as our heart remains open to serve the truth. What's important is that we strive to understand and act in accordance with His blessed directive."

"I don't believe abandoning my own flesh and blood when he desperately needed me is one of His 'blessed directives.'"

"You keep saying you abandoned Thaddeus, but did you really? It may feel that way because of what happened, but if you thought for a second that he was in serious trouble, his life was in danger, or that suicide was even a remote possibility, what would you have done?"

"It shouldn't have taken that for me to go see him."

"But you would have gone."

Theodosius lowered his head. "Yes."

"That doesn't sound like abandonment to me."

Theodosius shuffled back to his recliner. He extended his hand to Vines and forced a brief mouth-only smile. "Thank you for coming."

Vines opened his mouth to speak, closed it, and shook hands. He extracted a few pamphlets, books, and other reading materials from his leather satchel and placed them on the coffee table. "Thank you for inviting me into your home. Call me anytime if you'd like to talk." He extended his arms. "Before I leave, can I offer a prayer?" Theodosius hesitated a moment then took his hands. The two men closed their eyes and bowed their heads.

"Dear God, your faithful servant Theodosius Trask is suffering. Please offer him the comfort and reassurance that only You can provide that he will overcome this pain. Grant him the strength and courage to forgive himself that which requires no forgiveness so that he may shed this black cloud and move forward with peace, serenity, and the joy that only You can bring. Amen."

Vines stepped back and offered Theodosius a warm smile. "Please think about what I've said. Call me anytime. I'll keep you in my prayers."

Bart placed his hand on Vines's shoulder. "Thank you so much for coming."

Vines shook hands with Bart. "You're welcome," he said softly. "Please keep me in touch."

As he began to leave, a man suddenly appeared on the front porch. Bart froze.

Before them, through the screen door, stood Anthony McInnis.

Bart slowly approached the door, staring with wide, searching eyes through the screen at the man he had tried to forget, the man who, with anger in his heart, had threatened him and ordered him out into a driving rain. Stung hard by a reawakening of bitter, painful memories, had Anthony McInnis now returned to exact his revenge in the name of long overdue cosmic justice?

Bart studied the man. The glowing hot anger Bart had previously seen in his eyes appeared to be gone. Did Bart now see a vague quiet pleading in those eyes? He couldn't tell. Anthony's lips seemed to be pressed together in contrition, or were they? His shoulders, previously straight, were slightly hunched. What did it all mean? Was he trying to trick them? Bart glanced at his blazer. Could he be hiding a weapon?

"What are you doing here?" Bart asked brusquely.

Anthony spoke quietly, showing no emotion. "I'd like speak to your father."

"Why?"

"May I speak to him? Please?"

Bart studied his eyes. What were they saying? For a moment uncertainty paralyzed him, tightening his guts. Theodosius took a step toward the door, coming into Anthony's line of sight. "Who is it?"

Bart stepped between them.

Make a decision.

With every fiber of his body on high alert, holding his breath, Bart opened the door and stepped back, remaining between Anthony and his father. "Come in."

Anthony crossed the threshold. Vines headed for the door. Bart grabbed his arm without taking his eyes off Anthony. "Can you stay?" he asked with imploring eyes.

"Yes, of course."

Theodosius approached them. "Can I help you?"

"Are you Pastor Theodosius Trask?"

"Yes. Who are you?"

"My name is Anthony McInnis." He took a deep breath. "I was Thaddeus's partner."

Theodosius frowned, then his eyes shot open. He turned to his son.

Bart shook his head. "I had no idea he was coming."

Anthony stepped toward Theodosius. "I've come to speak to you."

"Who sent you here?"

"Can we talk, please?"

Theodosius stood still as a post, staring at him. With his insides convulsing Bart escorted Anthony to the couch. Vines grabbed a wooden chair from the dining room. Anthony sat up straight with his hands in his lap. "What I want to say to you ... some of it may not be easy to hear. I've not come to hurt you, but I think some of it will be hurtful. I'm sorry for that, but I have to say it all, truthfully, as I felt it then and as I feel it now."

Theodosius stared at him with disbelief in his eyes.

"I met Thad during our senior year in high school at a football game. At his insistence, our relationship had to be kept secret. The very notion of coming out terrified him, so I agreed to keep us on the down-low. It restricted us to phone calls and a few nights and weekends, but we made it work. I figured that in time we would somehow work it all out."

Anthony glanced at the Bible sitting on the coffee table. "I knew at the beginning about his strong faith. We didn't talk about it much, but I could tell he was struggling. One day, we finally talked. I told him straight out he had to stop feeling guilty about who he was. He tried so hard to believe that, but he just couldn't seem to break out of his terrible uncertainty over it all, between what the Bible said and what his intuition, his common sense, and his heart told him. I wondered out loud about whether it would be best if we broke it off. I'll never forget that look on his face. It was as if I had told him he had terminal cancer. He asked me not to give up on him. He said he needed just a little more time."

Bart listened and watched intently from the edge of his seat. Could he find anything in Anthony's words, tone, or facial expression that concerned him? Not yet. His father sat straight and rigid, locked on Anthony's eyes.

Anthony glanced briefly at Bart before continuing. "Two weeks later he came to see me. At first he couldn't even speak. Finally, he gave me the news I was dreading. He had decided to step away from the seminary and join Exodus. Our relationship would have to end. He said he had written me a letter telling me all this but decided to tell me in person. All he could say was 'I'm sorry,' over and over. Tears rolled down his cheeks. I was gutted. I asked him if he had spoken to anybody about this. He said he had just discussed it with you earlier that day.

Anthony flopped back onto the couch and looked up at the ceiling. "When the door closed behind him, I slumped to the floor, shaking, unable to think a single thought. Later, when the initial shock began to subside, all I could feel was anger for you. This was your fault. He was struggling with indecision, but you had put an end to that, hadn't you? At that moment, I wanted to kill you. If you had walked in the room at that time, looking for your brother, I believe I would have."

Bart jumped up. Theodosius raised his hand toward his son. Bart reluctantly sat.

"A month later I ran into him in the grocery store." Anthony closed his eyes and pressed his lips together. "He looked terrible—thin, pale, exhausted, looking ten years older. He gave me a smile, the saddest smile I've ever seen. I could barely speak. I asked him how he was. He said he was managing. I just stood there like a fool. That was it. When I got home I fell onto my bed and curled up in a little ball. I just lay there, grieving for him, and hating you.

"Over the years I've never forgotten the love I had for him and the hatred I had for you. Then, twelve days ago, out of the blue, your son came to see me, wanting to know more about the uncle he'd never met and if I could help you. He tried to explain it all, but I shut him down. All I could see and hear and feel was my anger for you, fresh and raw as on the day Thad died. I kicked him out and tried to forget the whole thing but then, yesterday, just when the shock of his visit was beginning to wear off, Jennifer Adams showed up."

Bart straightened. "What? Jenn went to see you?"

"Yes, with guns-a-blazing. I told her to get lost, but she wouldn't go. I slammed the door in her face, but she just kept knocking. I told her I was going to call the cops, but that just made her knock louder, so I finally let her in. I told her she had five minutes before I would throw her out the window. She said I had no right to blame you for Thad's death and that I should help you. She said a Pastor Jeremy Vines, founder of the Reformation Project, was going to be visiting today at two, and that I should go." Anthony turned back to Theodosius. "I laughed in her face. I said of course you're to blame. Thad adored you. He may have had his own uncertain notions, but he obviously got his final marching orders from his big brother."

Theodosius glanced at his Bible and shut his eyes.

"Well, she talked my ear off, telling me how unfair that was, how I had a chance to change your mind about homosexuality, and how that could affect a lot of people. Didn't I want to support that? I told her sure, I'd support that, but I'd rather get hit by a train than lift a finger to help you."

Bart sprang up. "I've heard enough. I'm going to ask you to leave now."

Theodosius turned toward his son. "Sit down, Bartholomew," he said quietly.

Bart stood frozen, as if having not understood his words.

"I said sit down!"

Bart dropped onto the chair as if he'd been shot. He texted Jennifer.

You saw McInnis??? He's here. Catastrophe! Get over here ASAP.

Anthony glanced at Vines. "When I said that to Jennifer, about not helping you, she gave me such a look; it shot right through me. She said what a shame it was that I had the chance to give Thad's death some meaning, to have some good come from it, but refused to do it, because I couldn't see past my own hatred. Before I could answer, she'd left.

"I just sat there, shell-shocked. I pulled out a great big old box, buried in the back of my closet, containing his personal effects and old photos. The day he died I filled that box and taped it closed with enough duct tape to survive a nuclear blast. Every time I moved, I took it with me, never thinking I'd ever have the courage to open it. I guess the time had finally come."

Anthony smiled wistfully. "I picked up his watch, his glasses, his hat, his old Bible—worn leather cover, almost every page dog-eared. I just held them in my hands. I smelled the hat, pretending after all these years it still contained his scent. I pulled out a couple of small photo albums. I hadn't seen those photos for thirty years. I put the albums back in the box and was about to seal it up, probably for the last time, when something caught my eye."

Anthony extracted from his jacket pocket an envelope with his name on it. "I had found this at the back of his desk drawer half buried in paper on the day he died. I knew what it was, of course—the 'Dear John' letter he said he'd written to me. I couldn't possibly read it back then, so I threw it into the box. This time I opened it." He extracted a letter from the envelope and held it out for Theodosius. "I'd like you to read it."

Theodosius shook his head forcefully. "No."

Anthony opened the letter.

My dearest Anthony-

I write this as a pathetic replacement for telling you, in person, that which I can't seem to find the courage to say to your face. After much quiet reflection, soul searching, and prayer, I have made the decision that I can no longer continue as a gay man committed to the Word of my Lord and savior, Jesus Christ.

Today I made the decision to leave seminary and enroll in Exodus, an organization dedicated to breaking the curse of homosexuality and bringing God's children back to the kingdom.

My broken heart will miss you more than I could ever say. I hope with all my being that you can understand this, accept this, and give me your blessing. I have not yet spoken to anyone about my homosexuality. If I can find the courage, I plan to tell Theo when I see him next week. At this point I don't feel I have the strength to tell my parents.

In the end, I must cling to the teaching of Jesus, and no matter what the challenge, stand with the divinely inspired Word.

With great love,
Thaddeus

Anthony handed the letter to Theodosius. "Is this his handwriting?"

Theodosius stared at the paper with wide glassy eyes. "Yes, but I don't understand—"

"Check the date in the top right corner. What does it say?"

"August twenty-first."

"What day did he talk to you?"

"September first."

"Are you sure?"

"Yes, he told me on the day before his birthday, September second. I'm sure of it."

Anthony nodded. "This was written eleven days *before* he spoke to you, *before* you thought he was asking for your advice, *before* you even knew he was gay. He had already made his decision before seeing you. He said it himself, in the letter."

"But if he'd already made up his mind…?"

"Why didn't Thaddeus just tell you what he'd decided? We both knew him well enough to know the answer. You were his big brother, his confidante and advisor in all things big and small. For him to tell you he'd already made the biggest decision of his life before discussing it with you, even if he knew you'd agree, that would be like slapping you in the face. He didn't tell you, because he wanted you to feel included in the decision, that your input *mattered* to him, even if it wasn't going to change a thing."

Anthony stood. "Do you see what this means? We've both been wrong about this. You didn't lead him to this. You didn't make his decisions. You didn't even put these ideas in his head. Your guilt, my anger … we've both been carrying it on our backs all this time. The time has come to let it go. I have. Now it's your turn."

Theodosius stared at the letter. "I had no idea. When he told me, I thought he wanted my advice."

"Of course you did because he'd always asked you about the big stuff. For him, sharing his biggest issues with you was his way of showing you respect, even love."

Theodosius fell back into his recliner, clutching the letter.

"Pastor Trask, you didn't push him into anything."

"Yes, but...."

"But what?"

"It doesn't change the fact that if I hadn't abandoned him, he'd still be alive today."

"How *could* you have known he was in such bad shape?" Anthony asked, gesturing forcefully with his hands. "You called him. He said he was struggling but it would be okay. Am I right? He hid the depth of his true suffering well over the phone. It was different for me. I saw that suffering with my own eyes that terrible day in the grocery store, and I walked away. For the longest time after he had died, a day didn't go by when I wondered, if I hadn't walked away from him that afternoon, if I had insisted on reaching out to him, to help him get through it one way or the other, would he still be alive?" Anthony stepped toward Theodosius. "You talk about guilt? I've got guilt. I'm going to have to live with that until the day I die. I know you feel bad about not being there for him, but you couldn't have known what was going on. Guilt is such a terrible thing, especially when there's nothing to be guilty of. Please, it's time to let this go as well." Anthony touched his arm. "Look at me."

Theodosius lifted his head until he found Anthony's eyes.

"Theodosius Trask, this whole terrible thing, it's not your fault. Do you hear me?"

The screen door flew open. Jennifer burst into the room, out of breath. Theodosius turned toward her with a tsunami of silent grief in his eyes, freezing her in place just inside the door. The wind blew in the trees. The screen door groaned on its hinges. The room waited in stunned silence.

Theodosius lowered his head, clasped his hands, and closed his eyes.

Linda came down the stairs. She looked at Bart and nodded.

They crept out in silence.

Bart called Junia from the front lawn.

"… I'm telling you, the whole thing, it was surreal."

"I can't believe Jenn did that."

"Listen, I've got Anthony, Jenn, and Pastor Vines out here with me. Could we come over now, maybe just to sit on the back porch and take a breath?"

"Of course. How is Mom?"

"I'm not sure. He told her everything this morning. She was up in her bedroom listening. She came downstairs just as we were leaving."

"Come on over."

Bart turned toward the house. What had just happened? Pastor Vines and Anthony McInnis, with his astonishing letter, were nothing less than magnificent. Yet, for all that, that terrible look of grief….

A vague ache grew within him. Despite everything, his father still couldn't seem to shake his anguish. Should Bart have allowed himself to expect otherwise? He knew as well as any psychologist, philosopher, or sage that changing a person's deepest convictions, the lifeblood of their emotional survival, is enormously difficult, but he also believed that change was possible—it had to be—if only the very strongest case could be made. Somewhere, he must have gone wrong, but where?

Bart turned to Vines. "Did you see his face when we left? I just don't know what else to do."

Vines laid his hand on Bart's shoulder. "Can I give you a word of advice?"

"At this point, I'll take anything."

"Be patient. The kind of change we're looking for comes in all shapes and sizes. Sometimes it can happen in a flash, but usually the change that lasts, if it's going to happen, it takes time, care, and nurturing."

"I hear you, but we have an emergency here."

"Please be patient."

"If we need you, can I call?"

"I'll come running."

Bart approached Jennifer. "I can't believe you went to see him."

She shrugged. "It just came over me. I had to try."

"How did you find him?"

"Same as you. I had his name and the city. That's all I needed."

On the way over to Junia's place, Bart called Sarah. She answered on the first ring.

"How'd it go?"

"I don't really know. My head is about to blow off. We had an unexpected visitor."

Bart hurriedly recounted the astonishing events of the afternoon as he pulled into Junia's place.

Sarah switched the call to video. Her eyes flew wide open. "Wow! I wish we knew what he was thinking."

"Listen, I've got to go. I'll call you later."

They sat around the large patio table on Junia's back porch. She brought out a six-pack of beer.

Bart looked into the house. "Where's my boy?"

"Sleeping."

As he lifted the bottle to his lips, his phone rang.

Bart sprang off his chair. "Mom, is everything okay?"

"James just got back into town from his conference. Are you still with the others?"

"Yes. Why?"

"Your father wants to see you, all of you, at seven o'clock. Is the pastor still with you?"

Bart frowned. "Yes. What's going on?"

"Can you come back, all of you?"

He glanced at the group. "Yes, of course. We'll be there."

James and his father stood on the front porch. Theodosius met them at the bottom of the stairs. Bart looked into his father's eyes. Theodosius glanced at his son, emotionless. He began walking toward the church. "Can I ask you all to follow me?"

He led them to the sign in front of the church. This sign, constructed by Theodosius's grandfather, with its stone base and large rectangular carved oak frame, as old and sturdy as the church itself, had been the favored backdrop of many a family photograph during special occasions. Bart remembered his father once proudly stating that most of the townsfolk probably had a photograph of the famous sign in their family album.

A large white sheet covered the lettering. Bart exchanged a look of bewilderment with the others. Theodosius, standing off to the right of the sign, cleared his throat. "I have an announcement to make."

James removed the sheet. Theodosius read the words, written in script with large metal letters, as if reciting a speech to a large audience.

Grace Baptist Church of Traskville
Pastor Theodosius Trask
Worship Services Sunday, 10:00 a.m.,
Wednesday, 7:00 p.m.

"With this unveiling, I hereby take back my church from my son, James." He pointed to his name on the sign. "*I* am the leader of this church. From the day my father stepped aside, *I* have been its leader. *I* will continue to be its leader, in service of the people of this fine town."

Jennifer, standing in front of Bart just to the left of the sign, pointed to a large rectangular piece of cloth fastened with tape covering the left lower corner. "Looks like you forgot to remove this."

Theodosius turned toward the sign. "Looks like I did," he said flatly. "Can you please get that for me?"

With a flick of her wrist, Jennifer removed the tape holding the cloth. She suddenly froze. Her eyes sprang open.

Bart approached her. "Jenn, are you—" A jolt of electricity shot through him. Anthony and Pastor Vines crept toward the sign. Anthony caught his breath. His eyes suddenly filled with tears. He ran his hand over the words, formed from small letters. He spoke the words, slowly, deliberately.

"All Orientations Welcome."

Pastor Vines put his hands up to his mouth. Jennifer staggered back several steps, slumped to the ground, and began to weep.

Theodosius remained next to the sign, motionless and silent, looking out across the road. With tears in his eyes, Bart went to his father. "I ... I don't know what to say."

"You don't have to say anything."

"I just can't believe it. Are you sure about this?"

"Am I sure?" He looked at his son, straight-faced. "I'm sure enough."

"What did it? What convinced you?"

"Convinced me? You did, mostly, together with my reading and research."

"But you still seemed so uncertain, even after the pastor was done."

"I wasn't uncertain. I just couldn't accept it."

Bart shook his head. "So what changed?"

"It's a strange thing, but it didn't seem enough to just *know* it. Then Anthony McInnis appeared. I saw into his eyes, and I heard his story, and I felt his pain, and I ... I felt the love he had for Thad. I *felt* it. At first I was shocked. After you all left I just sat there, stunned, unable to think. But then, in the time it takes to ask and answer a simple question, everything suddenly changed." Theodosius glanced at Jennifer staring at the sign in disbelief. "I don't understand it, but ... how can a loving God deny this?"

Bart stared in stunned disbelief at his father.

Theodosius smiled, a bittersweet smile. "It's funny. I've always looked to the Bible, my enduring compass for life and living, for all the answers, and I suppose I'll never stop doing that. But this time it seems I needed a little extra help. This time, I found the answers elsewhere, in the heart of a man I'd never met until today."

"And that amazing letter."

"I had no idea. I'll always feel guilty that I didn't do enough to help my poor brother, but after listening to Andrew and Pastor Vines, at least I can now go on." For a moment they stood, heads bowed, staring at the trampled grass between them, saying nothing. Theodosius grasped his son's forearm. "None of this would have happened without you."

"I had a lot of help."

"Remember when you said to me on the veranda that despite our differences I inspired you to become a professor and follow your passion? That's really something for a father to give a son. Well, you've given me something too. You've made it possible for me to open my mind *and* my heart in ways I couldn't have imagined. For that, a thank you doesn't seem enough." Theodosius placed his hand on Bart's shoulder. "I'm sorry I've never told you, but I *am* proud of you, my son."

Bart tried to respond, but no words came. His eyes filled with tears.

"Please excuse me. I have a few other people to thank."

After thanking Pastor Vines, Theodosius turned toward Anthony and extended his hand. "Thank you for everything. I'll never forget you."

Anthony ignored the hand and gave Theodosius a hug. "I'm sorry for all the anger I had. Please forgive me."

"There's nothing to forgive."

Theodosius turned to Jennifer. "I'm so sorry. I owe you more than I can say."

"You've paid me back more than I can say."

Theodosius turned to the group. "I'm afraid I must leave you. I'd like to go into my church now. I've got a sermon to re-write."

They watched him sprint up the steps of the church and disappear inside. Pastor Vines, Jennifer, and Anthony said their heartfelt goodbyes to Bart and left in their cars, leaving Bart and James standing next to the sign.

Bart turned to his brother. "How are you doing with all this?"

James raised his eyebrows and took a deep breath. "To be honest, I'm not really sure."

"Good. That's a start. I know it can't be easy."

"We'll have to see what happens around here, won't we?"

"Yes, we will."

"When are you going back?"

"Tonight. I'm going to stay overnight with friends in Atlanta before meeting up with Sarah in Ashville for a couple of days. I won't be able to get back for a little while. Things are getting pretty crazy for me. Take care of the family, you hear?"

James forced a smile. "We'll do our best."

"That's all we can do." He paused a moment. "Hey, listen, I just want to tell you again, what you did that night.... There are some people in this world whom I've come to deeply admire, but you'll always be the real hero in my life."

James flushed. "Coming from you, that's a big deal."

Bart gave his brother a long tight hug, took a picture of the sign, and left.

As Bart drove away he replayed the events of the day leading up to that extraordinary moment in time when he saw those improbable three words, conspicuously small, yet larger and brighter and louder than he could have ever imagined.

Rolling down the all-too-familiar roads he opened the windows wide to see the trees and sky and feel the wind on his face. He knew they were the same trees and sky and wind he had seen and felt many times before, when his mind had been occupied by smaller things, but now they looked strangely different, almost as if they *knew* that something momentous had shaken the earth in a tiny corner of the world.

Against all odds a mountain had been moved, if only just a little. That this most improbable thing happened at all was astounding enough, but *how* it happened….

For as long as he could remember, Bart fervently believed that the dispassionate application of reason to evidence was humanity's *one and only* antidote to self-destruction. What else was there?

Anthony McInnis.

Astounding indeed.

As he drove down the long, straight single-lane country road, he heard the ringing of church bells in the distance.

He listened intently until the sound of the last ring faded into silence, as if having never existed, just like his voice over the years, momentarily capturing his father's attention but ultimately fading into thin air without a trace.

Bart permitted himself a measured smile.

Not this time.

This time, defying all reasonable expectations, his voice of change, together with the impassioned pleas of others, had found an opening, a tiny crack in an impenetrable wall of certainty through which light could enter.

He shook his head in happy amazement.

The air turned cooler. The trees announced the arrival of a brisk breeze. Gun-metal gray clouds filled the sky. A light cool rain began to fall, yet, at least for a few minutes, sharp streaks of sunlight continued to touch down from low in the sky, creating a strangely beautiful pattern of light and dark. The rain, wetting his face and hair, felt quite wonderful.

What would happen now? Would the sliver of light grow, or in the second it took to blink, vanish as if never present? He knew, all too well, that this was also possible.

All he could do was his best.

As the intermittent drizzle and dusk gave way to a driving rain, shiny silver streets, and darkness, Bart closed the window, sped up the windshield wipers, and called Sarah.

About the Author

Dr. Gary McCarragher was born in Montreal, Quebec, Canada. He received his medical training at McGill University and enjoyed a successful career as a gastroenterologist in the Tampa Bay area before becoming a hospice physician in 2009. As part of his passionate advocacy for hospice, Gary has published multiple newspaper articles on hospice care. Gary also enjoys the arts and music and has performed in community theater, where he received an award for Best Actor. *Revelation* is his third novel.

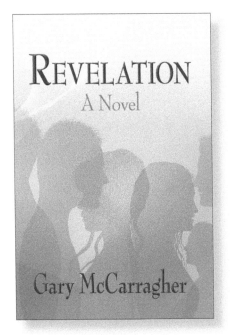

Revelation
A Novel
Gary McCarragher

www.GaryMcCarragher.com

garymccarragher@gmail.com

Also available in ebook format

TO PURCHASE:

Amazon.com

BarnesAndNoble.com

SDPPublishing.com

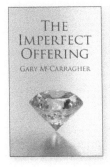

Other books by
Gary McCarragher:
The Imperfect Offering
Unhinged

SDP Publishing

www.SDPPublishing.com
Contact us at: info@SDPPublishing.com

Ingram Content Group UK Ltd.
Milton Keynes UK
UKHW011819030423
419563UK00001B/376